Ritual Sacrifice
An Illustrated History

BRENDA RALPH LEWIS

SUTTON PUBLISHING

First published in the United Kingdom in 2001 by
Sutton Publishing Limited · Phoenix Mill
Thrupp · Stroud · Gloucestershire · GL5 2BU

British Library Cataloguing in Publication Data
A catalogue record for this book is available from the British Library.

ISBN 1-7509-2707-0

Title page photograph: Aztec sacrificial knife. The Aztecs were not without a certain grim humour, here linking sex with death. The photograph is of a modern tourist replica. (*H.R. Lewis*)

Typeset in 12.5/15 pt Garamond.
Typesetting and origination by
Sutton Publishing Limited.
Printed and bound in England by
J.H. Haynes & Co. Ltd, Sparkford.

Contents

List of Illustrations

Colour plates
Between pages 54 and 55

An offering to Horus
Solar boat of Pharoah Khufu

Between pages 118 and 119
Hindu funeral pyre, Bali
Grave offerings, Sulawesi
Skull burial, Celebes Islands
North American skull rattles
Santerian altar
Burning of the Wicker Man
Nepalese 'sky burial'
Shinto offerings
Suttee memorial, Jodhpur
Ritual cleansing by the Ganges
The goddess Hevajira
Offerings for sale at a Hindu temple
Jain fire ceremony
Taiwanese fire prayers
Puja offerings, Khatmandu
Dayaks of Borneo sacrifice a cockerel
Women make flower offerings, Orissa

All pictures unless otherwise credited are © 2001 Corbis®.

With special thanks to Chris Barwick at Corbis Professional Licensing, London. e-mail sales.uk@corbis.com or free phone 0800 731 9995.

About Corbis Images

Based in Seattle USA, Corbis® is a worldwide source for digital images. Some 65 million images are currently searchable, over two million royalty-free. The collection includes news and sport, classical reportage, travel, fine art, history, world culture, celebrity portraits and commercial photography, including material from major institutions and private collections. For further information visit www.corbis.com

Introduction

The principle of sacrifice is as old as human consciousness. The development of human spirituality and an understanding of violent and unpredictable Nature went hand in hand with human evolution. However, whereas social mores, modes of thought, customs, traditions and other facets of cultural life have differed widely across the world, the basics of religion and sacrifice have remained very much the same. There was no need for contact and exchange of ideas or even awareness that any other communities existed as peoples all over the world formulated their beliefs by dipping into a global pool of concepts and practices that transcend time, place and lifestyle.

Even where environments have been radically different – the icy wastes of Siberia, for instance, and the burning deserts of Asia or Africa – the world was once seen to be alive with gods and spirits needing nurture and propitiation. If offered the right sacrifices, they would dispense aid and special favours. From this, ideas applied world-wide that these powers were due their share of successful hunts, harvests, fine craftwork or victory in battle. They would control the excesses of Nature, engineer the cycle of agriculture, ensure the continued availability of materials and fend off floods, volcanic eruptions and all other disasters. They could make human desires and needs into reality.

There was also a universal fear that unless these offerings were made to a very precise formula, then they would be invalid. To ensure perfection, peoples as far apart as the Romans, the Jews and the Chinese, for instance, followed minutely detailed instructions. At one stage in their long history, the Chinese even had a special government department that laid down every move, every gesture, every single word and every syllable involved in their sacrificial ceremonies.

Likewise, the burnt offering was a common form of sacrifice. So were omens and divination as an adjunct to sacrifice, the status of blood as the greatest and most efficacious offering, the sacrifice of the gods themselves to obtain their power and the special place in sacrifice of the first-born son in families.

This last concept arose even in Christianity, which never required physical sacrifices in worship, and waged many wars against the pagans who did. Jesus Christ, regarded by Christians as the only sacrifice that would ever be required by suffering humanity was, after all, the firstborn son of God. There does, however, remain an ancient sacrificial echo in the Catholic belief in transubstantion, the idea that the body and blood of Christ become physically present in the wafer and the wine ingested at Holy Communion.

All over the world, too, gods and spirits were seen as much like human beings, with appetites, moods and ambivalent characteristics. The Hindu gods of India could be both good and evil. Shiva, for example, is both creator and destroyer of worlds. In Greek mythology, the gods lived in a complex interrelationship with humans, frequently intervening to produce offspring whose god-like status was tempered by human frailties. Jehovah, the God of the ancient Hebrews, later enlisted as the God of Christianity and Islam, was capable of great munificence and terrible anger.

All gods needed to be fed and had to receive their portions of food and meals, or they were fed metaphorically by the devotion, obedience and self-sacrifice of their adherents. Sacrifice could be actual or symbolic, set in faiths with many gods or only one. Nevertheless, the relationship with humans has always been the same: humans obeyed and the gods were benevolent, humans disobeyed and punishment and revenge would follow.

Although sacrifice today is not so common as it was in former times, and those who attempt it can sometimes find themselves in court charged with cruelty to animals, the sacrificial urge as such is still present. At least in the western world, people have increasingly turned to the appeasement of secular gods as the power and importance of religion have declined. Casualties in warfare have long been regarded as a 'necessary sacrifice' towards political or territorial ends or for the attainment of victory. The phrase 'the supreme sacrifice' has been routinely used to describe death in battle for the sake of King and Country.

However, today, neither war nor religion is necessary to occasion sacrifice. Commerce and sport have adopted this mantle. Job cuts, redundancies or factory and mine closures have become new forms of sacrifice, usually for the sake of greater commercial efficiency. On an individual basis, football club managers are routinely fired when they fail to inspire their teams to sufficient success. Government ministers have sometimes been known to resign over misdemeanours committed within their departments. Members of Parliament have been forced to apologise for uttering opinions not in tune with their party's policy. Society demands these 'sacrifices' to ensure that whatever has gone wrong 'cannot happen again'.

Increasingly, science, technology and materialism emphasise that success comes from within the individual rather than being bestowed from above. According to Bishop John Robinson, author of the controversial *Honest to God*, published in 1963, God is no longer the frightening father-figure of the Bible, demanding obedience which, if not given, provokes instant penalties. This is a significant change in the concept of God as held by most religions up to very recent times. Long before Robinson, the German philosopher and Lutheran pastor Friedrich Nietzsche went even further and declared that Heaven was empty. God has gone away if, in fact, he was ever there. These are revolutionary ideas. So, too, is the concept that the ultimate goal of human existence is the ability to face up to reality without softening the blow by calling in divine aid. Humans, in other words, have thrown away their spiritual crutches.

It is possible that these new beliefs mark the final transition from dependence on deities and spirits to a new brand of self-confidence and the urge to chart a course through life that does not have to be divinely ordained. However, it is also possible that a majority of human beings have not yet reached this stage and may never do so. There are many millions of people, mostly in the Third World, who remain vulnerable to the depredations of Nature, whose economic base is fragile, whose education is rudimentary and who have no other power to turn to but God for hope of rescue from disaster. While, in the developed world, neopaganism is a growing belief, hinting at the dissatisfaction and even alarm many people feel at the apparent desacralization of the natural world. In this context, reliance on a God or gods is still a powerful force in the world, and a force still deemed to require its rituals and sacrifice so that life may continue and flourish.

1

The Nature of Sacrifice: An Overview

Earth has always been a terrifying place in which to live and the idea of making sacrifices to propitiate its fury is as old as human life itself. First personalized into gods, then into more spiritual beings resembling humans, but infinitely more powerful, Nature's potential to assault and destroy has been humanity's perennial predicament. For thousands of years, offering sacrifices to appease these furious forces was humanity's only answer.

The idea that all misfortune had its origin in the supernatural world – whether it was disease, drought, famine, floods, volcanic eruptions or any other calamity – was recognized wherever people lived close to Nature and its depredations. Seeking for reasons, the conclusion was that some offence had been committed to endanger the relationship between humanity and the gods. Disaster was not only punishment, but signalled a break in the system that governed life on Earth. It also seemed evident that the gods were perpetually angry, and were unlikely to turn beneficent without prompting. Sacrifice, however, had three-fold benefits: it could wipe out the offence, please the gods and spirits and restore the divine connection.

The modern scientific world has, of course, abandoned such ideas and relegated them to the realm of ignorance, backwardness and superstition. In doing so, science and technology have changed the ancient relationship between Nature and humanity. The modern imperative is to challenge and 'conquer' Nature, not tremble at its powers, perform rituals and so hope to avert its anger. Scientific cures for

1

disease, engineering and aviation achievements, television, computer, nuclear and other technology, the unlocking of the Human Genome, the exploration of Space – all these in some way confront the 'natural' order and enable humans to perform feats Nature never intended. Even where the natural forces triumph, through destructive earthquakes, floods or other disasters that destroy homes, lay waste villages or cities and ruin lives, the basic quest is always to find some means of curbing their excesses, solve the problem and put Pandora's ills back in their box.

In modern society, therefore, the background against which religion and its sacrifices and rituals came to hold such a central place in the ancient world has lost its relevance. Among the 'advanced' western societies at least, humans need no longer feel helpless before the fury of forces they cannot control. Fatalism – the acceptance of whatever hand destiny might deal – is no longer the only option. For many, this is what is meant by 'progress'. For others who distrust this definition and find its implications unnatural, humanity has distanced itself from what was once its proper place in the world.

In this context, the age-old concept of humanity as part of Nature and destined to live in harmony with it, persists today only among those traditional peoples who, knowingly or unknowingly, have stood aside from modern scientific developments. Some tribes living deep in the Amazon jungle, for instance, are not even aware that the world has vastly changed, outdating their way of life, their customs and their practices by many thousands of years. Some native Americans, Australian Aborigines, Pacific islanders or tribes in Africa and the more remote parts of northern Asia remain faithful to the world of their ancestors, honour the same spirits, observe the same taboos and perform the same rituals. The way of their ancestors is the only way they know, and to them, the ancient concept still holds good: Nature is the force that governs everything and, though frequently awesome, it is one that can be made bountiful by means of the right offerings and the right rituals.

This, though, was never a static idea and fatalism in the face of Nature was never entirely supine. It did not take long for ancient

Monumental head on the slopes of Nemrud Dagi, a volcano in Turkey, believed to be that of Zeus, the Greek sky god. These giant Hellenistic heads originally topped six statues over 10m in height, guarding the tomb of Antiochus I at the summit. Still listed as active, Nemrud Dagi last 'thundered' in 1441.

Adam Woolfitt

peoples to realize that it was possible to 'make deals' with Nature. However volatile, violent or vengeful they might appear to be, the gods and spirits could be pre-empted. By offering sacrifices on the 'in case' principle, it was possible to tap into the most overwhelming power in the world. In this guise, sacrifices could serve as means of winning divine favour for specific as well as survival purposes – to ensure a good hunt or harvest, to grant fertility or success in war, to ensure protection for the family or community, to preserve good health and strength and generally acquire what was most meaningful and necessary in life.

Sacrifices could also serve to give thanks, for example, after seeking the help of the gods in war and winning a victory. The gods, it was believed, were due a share of the booty, an idea that emerged quite strongly during the Bronze Age, which began around 7,000 years ago. A fundamental change in weaponry took place at that time as the discovery of metals expanded Earth's usable resources. Now, it became possible to forge weapons out of bronze and later, iron, both of which proved infinitely more durable and deadly than the wood or copper previously used. Consequently, archaeologists have discovered that many thousands of weapons were thrown as thanksgiving sacrifices into the ancient wells and springs where gods dwelt. When improving metallurgical techniques enabled alloy steel to be made from iron some 4,000 years later, the sacrifices became even more lavish, as quantities of weapons, even more vast, were thrown into swamps, lakes and rivers.

Other inanimate sacrifices could take almost any form depending on location. People offered what they had or what was most easily available. Native Americans offered furs, tobacco and food. In Inca Peru, offerings consisted of llamas, guinea pigs, coca leaves, maize and other food, gold and silver ornaments, carvings or feathers. Elsewhere, crops, incense, flowers, fruit, water and even wine were sacrificed. Together with milk, honey, oils, and beer, water and wine were classified as libations essential to life and health.

Water had a particular place in the business of sacrifice, as the indispensable source of all organic existence. Wine sacrifice was hardly less significant. In ancient times, wine was considered the 'blood of the grape' and doubled as the 'blood of the earth' from which the vines sprang. Wine therefore acquired its own spiritual, life-renewing status.

Regeneration was vital among agricultural communities which deified the Earth as the fount of all survival. Farmers soon perceived the rhythm of the seasons, with death in autumn and winter, rebirth in spring and the flourishing of life in summer. This was a pattern neither humans nor animals could emulate. They simply aged or succumbed to some disease or accident and died. For them, there was no going back. The agricultural cycle, however, was a continual process of going back and performing the same processes year after year after year. Little wonder, then, that the cycle acquired an aura of magic that permeated crops, vegetables, trees and everything else that grew from the ground.

The ultimate ritual in the business of regeneration was the sacrifice of the gods themselves. All round the world, mythologies contained accounts of Creation that include this idea. In the myths of ancient Persia, for instance, Zurvan, god of time and fate, acquired a son to create the world by offering sacrifices for a millennium. Likewise, in ancient Mexico, Aztec myths told how the gods sacrificed themselves in order to create the Sun, a selfless deed re-enacted in Aztec human sacrifice.

When the Spanish conquistadors first arrived in Aztec Mexico in 1519, they were sickened by the scenes of wholesale carnage they witnessed at the sacrificial altars of the capital, Tenochtitlan, and elsewhere in the vast Aztec Empire. What they saw was bloodletting on a scale well beyond what was permissible, or even thinkable, in Europe. What they did not understand – or in many cases seek to understand – was that this was not just the atavistic cruelty of godless savages. For the Aztecs, human sacrifice and the subsequent offering of hearts and blood were imperative if the Sun, which kept their world in existence, was to survive.

Aztec society was so thoroughly infused with this principle that it was considered an honour to serve as a sacrifice, since it transformed 'victims' into gods and assured them of a place in the heaven reserved for heroes. As Christians, with no place in their faith for such practices, the Spaniards were utterly puzzled when some Aztecs they saved from the sacrificial knife demanded to die on the altar and so fulfil their perceived destiny. The same mentality marked the response of a Brazilian who, when his sacrifice was prevented, concluded that his life had no meaning now that he could not be offered to the gods and afterwards eaten.

Blood had another, equally fundamental significance in the sacrifice scenario. It was recognized as the major life-force of human beings, which was why ancient agricultural societies used to perform human sacrifice in order to feed the gods and the earth. In Africa, ancient

America and elsewhere, this form of sacrifice was used to give regenerative meaning to the aging process of kings. These kings were not regarded as ordinary beings, even though they lived, sickened and died like everyone else. Great *mana*, or sacred powers, were ascribed to them, but when they grew old, these powers declined.[1] This, in turn, endangered the well-being of the tribe, the continuation of their crops and therefore the very survival of a king's subjects. Rectifying this situation meant, in effect, killing the king so that his powers could be renewed and strengthened in a more vigorous successor. Once the deed was done, the king's blood was mixed with seedcorn and the belief was that this made the corn abundantly fertile.

The death of kings could be the occasion for human sacrifice in quite another way. Belief in life after death was common in ancient religions. The afterlife, it was thought, was much like life on Earth. Consequently, in Mesopotamia, China, Japan or ancient Egypt, entire retinues of servants, warriors and other royal attendants would be buried, sometimes alive, with a dead monarch. This would ensure that he was properly attended in his next life. In Japan this practice died out by the sixth century AD, due mainly to the pacific influence of Buddhism, but it still occurred in China for another thousand years or more. The sacrifices were normally criminals or slaves, but prisoners captured in war also figured in these rituals. In Africa, the slaves of deceased kings might be buried alive with their dead master, or they were first killed, laid out in the bottom of the royal grave, and the king's corpse was placed on top of them. The fact that the royal and the eminent were also buried with a mass of belongings – furniture, jewellery, clothing, weapons – increased the image of an important newcomer to the afterlife.

The next world, the repository of dead souls, was widely viewed as a staging-post on the way to the gods. Among its inhabitants were ancestors who, it was believed, could serve as intermediaries. Ancestors were themselves worshipped in many cultures, from Africa to the Pacific, among the peoples of the ancient Mediterranean and Europe and most notably in India, China and Japan. This widespread distribution has persuaded some scholars that most sacrifices were made to ancestors. If so, it would not have been surprising. Dead ancestors were believed to live in close contact with the gods, which gave their intercession an added value. There was virtually no end to the requests that could be made of the ancestors, and no limit, either, to the reasons for offering sacrifices. The purpose might be to atone for wrongdoing, obtain a favour or blessing, ensure good fortune or some other desired benefit or seek protection against disease and help in producing good crops.

The relationship between the generations of a family did not cease with death. In death, ancestors were supposed to feel the same concern for their families they had shown while they were alive and were just as anxious to promote their wellbeing. The offering of sacrifices was, of course, the only feasible means of making contact with them and the only way of propitiating them should they become displeased.

There was, nevertheless, a hierarchy of ancestors that made some better prospects for sacrifice than others. If they had been lowly placed in life, ancestors received worship and sacrifice only from their nearest relatives. Some were not worshipped at all, since they were thought too unimportant to extract favours from the gods or deliver the benefits they had to dispense. Others, like the heads or founders of families, or a particularly wise man or woman, might be worshipped by entire communities and raised, in their estimation, to the status of gods in their own right.

Direct appeals to the gods through sacrifice could also be made, either in the absence of ancestor-worship or as an adjunct to it. Methods included libation, the pouring out of sacrificial wine or other liquid and the ritual spilling of blood, but there was another common practice – sacrifice by burning. There was a certain finality, a ritual commitment, in the destruction of a sacrifice by fire, and symbolic significance in the smoke as it curled towards the sky and so made contact with the gods.

Burnt offerings played a major part in ancient Greek and Jewish sacrifice and, for the Babylonians, there was no other way. All sacrifices were taken to Heaven by their fire god, Girru-Nusku, the intermediary between Heaven and Earth. Likewise, in India, Agni, the Vedic god of fire, brought humans into the presence of the gods after accepting their sacrifices.

Burnt offerings were, for obvious reasons, considered more suitable for the celestial gods, but in ancient Greece they were not thought appropriate for sacrifices to vegetation and fertility gods like Dionysius or Demeter. These ancient Greek sacrifices were known as *apura hiera*, or fire-less sacrifices. In Vedic practice, the same sacrifices could be made to all the gods, but the location was different: for the celestial gods, sacrifices were placed on a raised altar; for the earth gods they were placed on the ground. In ancient Greece, sacrifices intended for the gods of the underworld were buried, though they were sometimes burned either there or in a trench dug in the earth. Sacrifices to the water gods were similarly direct: humans or animals intended as offerings were drowned in lakes or rivers, and among the Norse Vikings of Scandinavia, they were thrown over cliffs to land in wells or waterfalls.

There was also a much simpler way of offering sacrifices, by placing them on a table or a mat and leaving them there for the gods to collect. In Ancient Egypt, this ceremony in which food and drink were left for the gods was termed 'performing the presentation of the divine oblations'. It took place every day. A daily sacrifice was also made among Hindus, this time comprising consecrated vegetables and rice, which were afterwards distributed among worshippers. In ancient Israel, priests and, after them, the laity, received the food sacrifices of the 'table of the shewbread' or the 'bread of the presence of God'. Consumption, however, was not part of Ancient Egypt and Greek practice in this form of sacrifice, though if the food disappeared after it was offered, the culprits were likely to be priests or attendants at the temple.

In many religions, priests or those appointed by God for the purpose were the most prominent among those responsible for the making of sacrifices, but before the development of priestly castes, the heads of households or the elders of a tribe were considered best qualified to make sacrifices. This was the case, for instance, in China where there were no professional priests. Apart from the paterfamilias, the only other individual with the right to make offerings was the king or emperor, who conducted the state sacrifices. Similarly, among the Aborigines of Australia, those thought most suitable to lead the acts of sacrifice were old men, who had acquired authority and deep understanding of tribal traditions. This occurred, for instance, among the Ila tribe of Zambia in situations of 'emergency' sacrifice when divine intervention was needed to transform an unsuccessful hunt. The oldest man among the hunters would lead the prayers for divine aid and, once a successful kill had been made, he led them again in offering meat as a thanksgiving.

However, the aged and eminent did not have a monopoly of sacrifice. In Vedic practice, it was possible to earn the right to make sacrifices by performing certain rituals. The complexity and severity of these rituals indicate that a proper state of grace had to be acquired before a sacrifice could be made. In this context, making sacrifices was itself a sacred act and would-be 'sacrificers' had to be purified before they were fit for contact with the sacred world.

Purification began with the *diksa*, or initiation, which required ritual bathing, followed by a time spent in seclusion for fasting and prayer. The idea was to remove all traces of the ordinary world, which could prevent the sacrifice achieving full potency and possibly offend the gods. After diksa, a 'sacrificer' became detached from the world of the profane. After the sacrifice was made, the process took place in reverse. He or she was returned to their former, ordinary, status by another ritual bath to wash away all traces of sacred power which may have become attached to them.[2] This and other, similar rites clearly underlined the basic meaning of the word 'sacrifice', which came from the Latin, to 'make sacred'. It has been suggested that every act of sacrifice was some kind of consecration and that a sacrifice performed outside specially sanctified places was a meaningless killing.[3]

It has been possible, this far, to formulate a universal explanation for sacrifice, but 'this far' has not proved far enough. What remains elusive

9

is a single theory that can explain why sacrifice rather than some other rite arose in the first place. This has not been for want of trying. An early idea, suggested in 1871 by the British anthropologist Sir Edward Burnett Tylor, was that sacrifice was a gift to the gods: this served the dual purpose of winning divine favour and calming divine anger. Sacrifice as a way of creating communion between a people and their gods was suggested by the Scots scholar William Robertson Smith in 1886. This was a more complex theory than Tylor's, involving a sacrificial meal where communion was established by those who shared food and drink in which the god is present.

Smith's theories also involved a totem which acted as the sacred symbol of a tribe and had a spiritual connection with it. A totem could be a plant or animal. Normally, it was taboo to eat the flesh of a sacred animal, except on special occasions when it was consumed to reinforce its connection with the tribe. When the animal was sacrificed, this was thought to create a union between the worlds of the sacred and the profane.

A different theory, and an attempt at an all-embracing definition, was the quest of Adolf E. Jensen, a Danish anthropologist who started with the problem of why glorifying the gods required sacrifice at all. Jensen found his solution in a myth of the Dema deities, who were the ancestors of the Marind-Anim tribe of southern New Guinea. Jensen, however, believed that the Marind-Anim were not the only descendants of the Dema deities: the entire human race was descended from them. Long before Man, in the far-distant primal past, the Dema lived on Earth and the start of human history was brought into being when one of the deities was killed. The crops that grew from the body of the dead deity became sacrifices when they were eaten. To Jensen, sacrifice was therefore a repetition of this mythological event.

For Sigmund Freud, the father of psychiatry, this re-enactment had quite another explanation: it was atonement for a son, who had been driven by the Oedipus complex to kill his own father. Full of remorse for this act, the son sacrificed an animal, hoping to reconcile and commune with the dead man through this other victim.

More recently, Richard Dawkins, author of *The Selfish Gene* published in 1976, has proposed 'memes' as an explanation for religion and with that, sacrifice and other rituals. According to Dawkins, memes are the cultural equivalent of genes. Genes, he writes, have a life of their own and use living bodies as a means of furthering their own survival. 'Natural selection', as proposed by Charles Darwin, did not take place within species, but within the genes, and just as genes control the human body, memes have the same effect on culture. Both become implanted in society, and in the case of memes result in the spreading of ideas such as patriotism, tastes in music or the arts, fashion and, of course, religion and sacrifice.

This concept of human beings as virtual captives of their own genes and memes became extremely controversial and has remained so, not least because Richard Dawkins is a well-known atheist. There have been strong religious objections to the idea that faith sprang not from spirituality or divine presence, but from the machinations of a cultural chromosome.

There have therefore been many opinions and many interpretations, but no universal agreement about the origin of sacrifice. This is not surprising when neither archaeology, which can provide some clues, nor anthropology, which seeks to unravel them, are exact sciences, with precise truths or self-evident facts. That alone is a valid reason why, this far, a satisfactory and universally acceptable answer to the question 'Why sacrifice?' has proved so hard to find.

2

The Birth of Belief: Sacrifice in Prehistory

The development of religious faith, and with it, the concept of ritual sacrifice, was the final step in the intellectual separation of humans from animals. When that occurred, between 130,000 and 30,000 years ago, in Neanderthal times, they were permanently set on different paths through life. Emotion, grief or loyalty, distinguishing characteristics of humans, were not absent from the mental make-up of animals, but their existence was basically instinctive, and their role was to live with Nature and accept whatever hand she dealt them. Meanwhile, a developing sense of awareness, an intelligent curiosity and an ability to tackle moral problems was leading humanity on towards spirituality.

The first signs of spirituality so far discovered occurred among the Neanderthals, who were cousins rather than direct ancestors of Homo Sapiens Sapiens, or modern Man. The Neanderthals were named after the Neander Valley not far from Düsseldorf in Germany, where the first remains were identified in 1856. Physically different from modern humans, and well-adapted to the climate of Ice Age Europe, Neanderthals had low and prominent brows, large teeth suited to tearing flesh, and heavy limbs. The large nasal cavity probably heightened the Neanderthal sense of smell, a vital attribute in a hunting culture.

At first, the Neanderthal remains were considered by some to be those of modern human beings who had died of some ghastly disease which distorted their bodies. Others, however, readily recognized the nearness to modern Man revealed by what was a truly sensational find at the time it was made. At that stage, the world stood on the brink of new knowledge of previously unimagined antiquity. The Neander Valley was only the start. Later excavations discovered Neanderthal remains at sites in France, Gibraltar, Italy, Iraq, the Ukraine, Uzbekistan, Croatia, and Israel as well as Zambia, Java in Indonesia, North and South Africa and Central Asia.

As the discoveries accumulated and the finds were interpreted, emotional, compassionate qualities were revealed. The Neanderthals cared for the sick and disabled. They practised a primitive form of religion and buried their dead with great care and some pomp. They seemed to regard death as another kind of sleep, which was why they arranged bodies in sleep-like positions, with knees drawn up and the head placed on a 'pillow' made of flint shavings or vegetation with a small piece of limestone underneath.

They were aware also of the principles of a higher power and the afterlife, to judge by the flint tools and implements found in some of their graves. These might have been placed there as equipment to be used in the next world, or as a guarantee of health and prosperity. In some burials, such as the Neanderthal grave discovered at La Chapelle aux Saints in France in 1908, recognizable hearths were placed around the bodies, a symbolic means, perhaps, of fending off the chill of death. Alternatively, the hearths could have been used to cook the funeral feasts which were part of the burial rites.

One of the most spectacular Neanderthal burials was found in the Shanidar Cave in Iraq where a one-armed man of around 40, who seems to have died in a rock fall about 46,000 years ago, was buried surrounded by flowers. These had been carefully, even artistically, arranged. Some of the flowers, which included yarrow, cornflower, groundsel, grape hyacinth and woody horsetail, had medicinal qualities, and it could be that these were the tools of the trade for a shaman or medicine man – a very important individual in Neanderthal and many other primitive societies.

Some of the evidence from Neanderthal burials appears to indicate that they observed rituals and sacrifice as part of the funeral rites. For instance, the burial of a boy aged about 12 discovered in 1938 at Tesik-Tash in southeast Uzbekistan revealed the horns of Siberian mountain goats planted in pairs around the grave, possibly as a protection. A grave at La Ferrassie, southwest France, excavated between 1909 and 1920, and in 1973, contained a man, a woman and six children interred close to each other.[1] Nearby, there were nine mounds, one of them containing the remains of a new-born child and three flints. The mounds, arranged in sets of three, were not accidental and the flints were not waste from tool manufacture: they were beautiful and shapely, obviously the result of careful chipping and not the sort to be carelessly thrown away. Elsewhere, burned animal bones were found in some graves, and in others, the remains of animals were discovered lying on the face or the body, probably as a sacrifice to the dead individual. There was also some magical significance in preserving the ribs of animals, their skulls, with vertebrae still attached, and the front legs of oxen or reindeer.

As more investigations were made, there was a build-up of information attesting not only to Neanderthal 'humanity' but to their use of ritual sacrifices and offerings. Deer antlers have been found on a child's grave at Qafzeh Cave in Israel, first discovered in 1933 and extensively excavated after 1977. The jaw of a boar was uncovered buried with an adult Neanderthal at the Skhul Cave, also in Israel, and excavated between 1929 and 1934. Both these finds have been fixed by Carbon-14 dating at around 100,000 years old.[2]

Animal sacrifices or offerings like those at Qafzeh or Skhul proved to be the most common type, but human sacrifice may also have been practised by Neanderthals. At La Ferrassie, a woman of 25 or 30 found buried in the grave of a man was not in a sleep-like position, but appears to have been tied up before interment. In addition, the family buried at the same site may well have died at the same time, for mass human sacrifice was not entirely unknown in ancient times.

There has long been a recognized connection between human sacrifice and cannibalism, and finds made in 1899 at a cave in Krapina, Croatia, uncovered some suspiciously dismembered remains which may

A collection of skulls from Neanderthal sites. The skull formation was distinct from that of our direct Homo Sapiens ancestors but the evidence suggests that Neanderthals organised socially, buried their dead with ritual ceremony and may have practised cannibalism.

indicate that eating human flesh was a feature of Neanderthal life and ritual. Some 20 people, men, women and children, were found, with cuts on their corpses resembling those Neanderthal hunters made on animals. The limbs were severed from the bodies and torn apart, presumably for the purpose of consuming the bone marrow. Yet, at the same time, the cave was full of animal bones, indicating that the hunting was good in the area, and that consuming fellow Neanderthals did not necessarily indicate a shortage of food.

Neanderthal findings have been controversial from the start, and there have been numerous rival interpretations, including the idea that Nature has been playing tricks by mimicking what appeared to be deliberate actions or signs of emotion and grief. In this context, the archaeologist Richard Gargett argued in 1987 that in all Neanderthal graves, the supposed ceremonial and cultural activities could have had

16

natural explanations.[3] Consequently, according to Gargett, the flowers in the Shanidar cave burial in Iraq could have been blown in by the wind or carried in by rodents building a nest in the cave. Similarly, a Neanderthal 'grave' found at Chapelle aux Saints in France in 1908 could have been formed by sediment falling on the cave-floor around the body and producing the appearance of a purpose-built burial place. At La Ferrassie, the nine mounds might have come about by the action of frost, which can create patterns as easily as an artificial arrangement. It has also been suggested that the goat horns found in the child's grave in Uzbekistan did not represent some kind of votive offering or protection, but were simply the means by which the grave had been dug. However archaeology and anthropology can be combative professions and theories can 'prove' anything.

Gargett's conclusions have been hotly disputed, not least by the English anthropologist Richard Rudgeley, who has championed prehistoric humans as the talented, innovative precursors of civilization rather than the shambling primitives of popular myth. One of the most disputed sites is at Monte Circeo, Italy, where a Neanderthal skull was found in 1939. The skull of the body found there had been severed from the spine in a way that allowed the brains to be drawn out and, presumably, eaten. This may have indicated sacrifice and cannibalism, but it is also possible that the brains were eaten by animals which had disturbed the body. Similarly, there could be more than one reason why, before burial, the flesh was stripped off the body of the 12-year old at Teshik-Tash and the same practice was used on a Neanderthal found in the Neander Valley: either this was a death ritual enabling other Neanderthals to eat the flesh and so gain the strength and courage of the individual concerned – a belief not uncommon in primitive societies – or the dead person was being disabled with a view, for example, to preventing his spirit from haunting other members of his group.

Rather more certain, though still not universally accepted, is the idea that the Neanderthals worshipped bears, which were potential rivals for cave-space and could be ferocious in asserting their rights. The rituals seem to have included the sacrifice of bears, maybe to a higher being who was believed to dispense food. The bear, surrounded by dancers, was killed by arrows or a spear-thrust into its lungs and its head, still attached to the skin, arranged over the body of a bear made out of clay. The most valuable parts – the head, the shanks, or the brains, the long bones and the marrow – were probably the most frequently used in sacrifice. This practice seems to have persisted among Siberian hunters of 11,000 years ago, in the Neolithic Age, and still lives on, symbolically, in the bear ceremonials practised in northern Europe and Asia and in North America.

A vast number of bear skulls and bones have been discovered in Neanderthal caves such as those at Drachenlock in Switzerland and some of the ways in which they were arranged suggest a ritual or magical purpose.

At Drachenlock, a large stone chest was found in a cave where Neanderthals lived, close to the entrance. Inside, the skulls of seven bears had been carefully arranged so that their muzzles faced the cave entrance. Further into the cave, there were six niches, each containing its own bear skull. Limbs were also found bundled together and a special 'structure' made up of the bones of four bears: two provided the base for a skull of a bear about three years of age, with the leg-bone of another, younger, bear piercing its cheek. Elsewhere, at Regourdou in southern France, the skulls and bones of about 20 bears were discovered in a rectangular pit, sealed inside by a huge stone slab weighing over a tonne. The orderliness of the bear discoveries points to something deliberate and a ritual purpose could well have been the explanation.

A much more convincing case of ritual sacrifice by Neanderthals occurred some 50,000 years ago when they dismembered a deer in a cave in Lebanon. The pieces were laid out on a bed of stones and sprinkled with red ochre, maybe as a symbol of blood. This has been interpreted as a sacrifice made to control the local deer population, either for the benefit of hunting or as an alternative way to preserve the animal in order to ensure the continuation of its species.

Sacrifices and rituals designed to conserve the animals hunted in prehistoric times were understandable acts of self-interest. This was one reason why, even after they became thinking, planning, knowing beings, humans could not entirely separate themselves from animals. They lived, after all, in a world where farming was as yet unknown, and animals were the prime, if not the only, source of food and survival. In addition, the hunt was an exercise in dangerous rivalry in which the hunted, not the hunter, appeared to have all the advantages – greater bulk, physical make-up that included weapons such as horns, hooves, large curved teeth or tusks, greater speed, infinitely more ferocity and much more strength. In this guise, animals, especially wild animals, were clearly beyond direct human control. By comparison, humans were physically puny, with soft skin that was easily pierced and a physique that could easily be disabled by heavy blows or by crushing. However, what humans did have was their nimbleness, an ability to employ guile, the brains to plan a hunt and the intelligence to carry out strategies – and another quality no animal possessed: the imagination to create a situation where humans could live in productive harmony with animals on the spiritual plane.

This was an idea which occurred automatically in the developing brains of the Neanderthals, which would one day take their human cousins into intellectual realms far beyond the reach of animals. A psychological residue remained from the primal past, in the continuing bond between animals and humans built up over many thousands of years of living together and competing for resources. To the hunter, this made the hunted not just creatures to be pursued, ensnared, killed and used, but beings with their own souls, attributes, personalities and affections and the same goal in life – survival.

It was an intimate connection eloquently expressed in the prehistoric paintings dating from about 17,000 years ago which were found in caves at Niaux in southern France, at Lascaux, one of five sites grouped close to each other in the Dordogne, and at the Chauvet Grotto, in southeast France, discovered by potholers in 1994. Chauvet contained images 31,000 years old, the most ancient known so far. In prehistoric cave art, human and animal forms were intermixed or humans were given animal characteristics. All this recalled a time when the ancestors of humans were little different from the animals who also wandered the world in search of food and shelter, and memories of that time were still pervasive. Once thought to be simply pictorial representations of hunting-magic, painted to ensure a good kill, prehistoric art carried an extra message – the attachment, despite the rivalry, of humans and animals.

The feeling of attachment was a major influence in the primitive faith known as animism, in which humans and animals were connected by magical and spiritual ties. Animals, it was thought, could be offended at being killed for food and other purposes, so that it became necessary to placate them and seek forgiveness. Fertility rites were performed and sacrifices offered for animals, and these, presumably, were meant to make up in some way for the deaths incurred in hunting. Hunters might rejoice when they returned home with a good kill that could provide their families with food, clothing, utensils and other necessaries, yet guilt and remorse were also present and had to be assuaged.

One custom which grew up was the preservation of an animal's skeleton or entire body or part of it. This may have been how the intact bodies of reindeer came to be sunk into lakes by hunting societies operating in the north of prehistoric Europe. Symbolically, this was not the sacrifice of an individual animal, but the sacrifice of the animal as a member of the herd to which it belonged. This procedure, which persisted in modern times among herding and hunting societies in north and central Asia, was intended to ensure the future of the reindeer or other species involved.

It was also meant to placate the 'Master of the Animals'. The 'Master', whose name was devised by nineteenth-century scholars studying hunter societies still surviving from ancient times, was a powerful supernatural spirit who was thought to protect game. He also exerted control over the numbers killed by making only a certain quantity available. If prayers, rituals and sacrifices were accepted, he would, hopefully, respond by leading hunters to places suitable for the kill. However, if animals were not killed with proper respect or the right rituals were not observed beforehand, the 'Master' could withhold

The bear cult was common among North American indians, as might be expected when bears and humans were competing for (and to avoid becoming) food. This bear 'totem pole' is from British Columbia.

Kevin R. Morris

prey. He would have to be pacified by sacrifices and prayers before he would change his mind.

The 'identity' of the 'Master of Animals' depended on the animals living in a particular area. In Europe and the adjacent areas of Asia, for example, the 'Master' was the bear. A reindeer assumed the role in the tundra of Scandinavia and northern Russia, while along the north coasts of Europe, Asia and Canada it was the whale, seal or walrus. This did not, of course, prevent the animal in question from being hunted and killed – that, after all, was a matter of survival, the most basic instinct living creatures possess. In prehistory, as in traditional societies which have survived virtually unchanged into the modern world, humans naturally responded to this instinct.

As the most valuable asset available, animals also figured as major sacrifices to gods who were not directly related to the business of hunting, but had an influence over it. The god of the sky, for instance, could create destructive storms, or pour down rain or produce drought by withholding it. Earth deities who 'owned' certain areas, such as lakes or forests, might fail to sustain the earth's fertility if sufficiently angered. If that were to happen, the vegetation or the supply of fish could be ruined, so robbing animals of their food. That, in turn, could spoil the chances of successful hunting to sustain the people.

However, all these misfortunes could be diverted by sacrifice and sacrifice on the grand scale was the purpose of the *mer*, a religious festival held every five years or so among the Cheremis and Udmurts of Russia. The meaning of *mer* was 'village community' and when the time arrived, several villages would attend to perform animal sacrifices to the gods of nature.

The site for some of these sacrifices was a grove of deciduous trees. These had sacred significance and were the places where the village ancestors had once worshipped. Here, white animals were sacrificed to the nature gods, and the accompanying prayers were made in a southerly direction. Conifer trees, too, had a supernatural aura, and it was in their vicinity, with prayers made towards the north, that black animals were sacrificed to the dead and the guardian spirits of the earth. These guardians watched over individual households as well as certain natural areas. Rituals and sacrifices for the dead were an occasion for venerating the ancestors who safeguarded family welfare and ensured the well-being and continuing prosperity of the family group.

A similar idea, that sacrifice could produce specific benefit, in this case a view of the future, also marked the horse-sacrifice ceremony practised among the ancient nomads of central Asia. Peoples, nomadic or otherwise, have always possessed a natural affinity with their particular methods of transport, and the horse had a monopoly that persisted from prehistory all the way to the development of motor cars in the late nineteenth century. For example, the peoples of Altai in the eastern part of Central Asia lived in an area of high mountains, deep valleys and dense forests, an arduous environment where horses were indispensable, not only for transport but also as pack-animals and, on occasion, as food.

The horse-sacrifice ceremony, which lasted for up to three days, involved a complex series of rituals in which a shaman made contact with the heavenly world and obtained important information: whether the next harvest would be successful, whether disease, epidemics or some other misfortune were imminent. Most vital of all, the shaman was able to learn how disasters could be averted by making sacrifices and what those sacrifices should be.

The ceremony began when the shaman released the soul of the horse, then chased and captured it. The horse was then killed and its flesh dismembered. Pieces of the flesh were offered to the spirits on the following evening and the shaman, accompanied by drums and chanting, symbolically rose to heaven on the soul of the horse. Physically, the shaman was ascending on a notched pole, a metaphor for climbing higher and higher into the heavenly plane. As he went, the shaman communicated the predictions for the future to his audience. Once these were concluded, there was much feasting, drinking and merrymaking as the people rejoiced in their new knowledge of how to assure their future. Five years later or more, they would return to receive further guidance and so the cycle of sacrifice and ritual would go on.

The effect of these repeated ceremonies was to infuse all aspects of everyday life with spirituality, since all aspects were under the scrutiny of some god or spirit which could turn malicious without warning. In this, the deities mirrored, or physically embodied, the forces of Nature in all their unpredictability: violent one moment, bountiful the next, smiling on the Earth and its inhabitants, then turning to furious acts of destruction by earthquake, storm, flood or fire. Much later, when Nature lost its divinity to the facts and formulae of science, the belief that rituals could fend off this exercise in power was labelled superstition. However, in the uncertain world of prehistory, and for a long time afterwards, Nature had to be confronted on an intimate, day to day basis, and always with survival at stake. In this context it was not unreasonable that every action in life and every contingency, should have its safeguard in sacrifice or prayer.

3

The Wrath of Yahweh: The Bible Lands

The civilizing influence of the Ubaidians, who arrived after about 4500BC in the area around the Persian Gulf later known as Mesapotamia, was greatly advanced some 1,200 years later by a semitic people who probably came from Asia Minor. These were the Sumerians, who brought with them architectural, organisational, technological social and cultural skills, including writing, that in time enabled them to make a quantum leap in the history of the world: prehistory was over and civilization – meaning 'living in cities' – was about to begin.

In time, the first known cities in Sumer were followed by many others, clustered around the banks of the Rivers Tigris and Euphrates in Mesopotamia. Ultimately, there were around thirty major cities occupying environments that varied between the temperate north, which had ample rainfall, and the much hotter and dryer desert lands of the south close to the Persian Gulf. It was only the two great rivers, and the ingenuity used by people in bringing them under control and making them work for the land through irrigation, that enabled these early cities to survive.

Mesopotamia was nevertheless a demanding place in which to live. This was not Egypt, the spoiled darling of the ancient world, where farmers only had to wait for the Nile floods to recede to be presented with fertile land. In Mesopotamia there was still good cause to fear Nature rampant, a force that was conceived, of course, as the wrath of the gods. They could cause droughts, pestilence, crop failure or the flooding or silting up of the rivers. When the River Euphrates burst its banks in around 4,000BC and flooded the Ubaidian city of Ur and its surrounding villages, the devastation was said to be comparable to the Great Flood. Little wonder, then, that religion and religious rituals in Mesopotamia reflected fear of Nature and the gods to such an extent that prayers and sacrifice were daily occurrences. One Babylonian temple kept 7,000 head of cattle and 150,000 head of other animal for sacrificial purposes alone.

It was the Sumerians who set the tone from the start. They believed that the human race had been created out of clay in order to relieve the gods of their workload. It followed that Man's destiny was to act as servants to the gods by means of offerings and sacrifices. These were also made to the spirits of the dead. These spirits, the Sumerians believed, existed in an 'afterworld', as ghosts: supplying them with food and drink would dissuade them from haunting the living. Coping with all this was an ongoing task. Apart from countless ghosts, there were more than 3,000 gods and goddesses of Sumer who between them controlled all aspects of life. In addition, inanimate objects, such as ploughs or building materials, had their own gods, and villages had their own local deities. Sumer was saturated with divine presence.

Food, and a great deal of it, was the most frequent form of sacrificial offering. Vast quantities of food, drink, meat, grain or entire meals were offered at Sumerian temples and at every ordinary meal consumed during the day. On feast days, there were banquets involving the sacrifice of numerous animals, mainly goats, sheep, cattle and birds and the burning of incense and aromatic woods. The divine portion of a sacrificed animal consisted of the right leg, the kidneys and a piece of meat for roasting. The rest was ritually eaten by the participants at the feast. In addition, libations of water were poured over sheaves of grain or bunches of dates in order to placate the gods of fertility and persuade them to grant rain.

Other offerings were graded according to their purpose. Mesopotamian temples acted as repositories for the divine 'property', so that items for use by the gods such as boats, beds, chairs or drinking vessels were taken into the temple treasuries. So were more exotic offerings such as jewels, ornaments and weapons acquired in the many wars that were a regular feature of Mesopotamian life.

The next category catered for individual offerings and sacrifices. Statues were made and placed before the image of the gods, so that the person represented could be seen in a permanent attitude of prayer, presenting gifts to the gods. The third type of sacrifice was the request for divine aid during illness. Models of arms, legs or any other part of the body were laid before the gods by sufferers from disease or disability so that a cure might be granted. Specialized sacrifices were made at some temples: at Eridu and Lagash, for instance, they consisted entirely of fish. Burnt offerings were confined to special sites – small, round altars or on the ground in special pans or trenches. These were in constant use, so much so that the ash piled up high and walls had to be built to stop it spilling over.

As Mesopotamia developed into a region studded with cities, the basic principles of the Sumerian faith, the Sumerian view of Man's purpose on Earth and the offering of daily sacrifices to the gods were handed down across the centuries. In Babylon, the most famous of all the Mesopotamian cities, the sacrifices of animals, vegetables, wine, beer, libations of water and the burning of incense were still extant well over a thousand years after the founding of Sumer.

Human sacrifice, which has often been seen as a substitute for cannibalism, was in a category of its own. It was not a regular practice in Mesopotamia, but more in the nature of a desperate last resort in cases of emergency.[1] The Second Book of Kings describes how the King of Moab, an area by the Dead Sea now in western Jordan, was in just such a situation in a war against the Israelites.[2] After being badly mauled in battle, he attacked with an élite force of 700 men in an effort to stem the Israelite advance, but failed. There was only one recourse now: the King sacrificed his eldest son 'who should have reigned in his stead . . . offering him for a burnt offering . . .'.[3] The desperate measure appeared to be successful: after the sacrifice, the Israelites withdrew.

The sacrifice of his own heir was the sacrifice of the most precious thing in a king's life – the son who would ensure the continuation of his dynasty. By extension, this also applied to other instances of dire calamity, such as an epidemic, or drought. In such situations, the Phoenicians, who lived in the area of present day Lebanon, used to sacrifice children to their god, Baal, and so did the Canaanites, the original inhabitants of ancient Israel.

Human sacrifice in ancient Mesopotamia included the mass burials of a royal household, a practice that also occurred in Ancient Egypt. In the city of Ur, the celebrated British archaeologist Sir Charles Leonard Woolley excavated more than 1,800 graves between 1922 and 1934. Woolley classified sixteen as royal tombs and found attached to them the mass burial places he termed 'death pits'. These tombs, where the Kings of Ur were interred with all their treasures, dated from around 2,700BC. Outside the doors of the stone houses containing the royal bodies, Woolley found the graves of their court officials, women and servants, both male and female, together with musicians and royal chariots, complete with charioteers.

The scenes in some of the tombs resembled tableaux of life as lived in the royal palaces. In the tomb of a woman named Pu-abi, one of her attendants was found crouched at her feet and another at her head. Twelve of Pu-abi's female attendants were grouped together and one of them had her fingers poised ready to play music on a large harp. Pu-abi was well guarded by five men, each of them wearing a dagger. They stood at the entrance to the burial pit. Nearby was a wooden sled, drawn by two oxen, with four grooms in attendance. Three more servants guarded a box which probably contained textiles, with gold, silver, copper, pottery and stone vessels surrounding it. There were models of lionesses, drinking tubes, swords, a saw and chisels, all fashioned in gold, together with an inlaid gaming board and mosaics made of shells. Also present were a large number of carved cylinder seals, a characteristic artefact of ancient Mesopotamia.[4]

Religion in the city of Ur, as elsewhere in Mesopotamia, centred on a pantheon of gods, although there was an element of monotheism here among cults who worshipped one chief deity. In Babylon, for instance, Marduk was the focus of faith. Dagan, possibly a weather or fertility god, was worshipped on his own throughout the Near East and especially in the area around the central Euphrates river. Further afield, in Phrygia in west-central Asia Minor, a cult specializing in the sacrifice of rams centred round Cybele, Mother of the Gods and her son Attis. After the ram sacrifice, worshippers bathed in its blood.

Although great powers were ascribed to these pagan deities, they were minor compared to the scope claimed for the god afterwards known as Yahweh or Jehovah. It was common practice in Mesopotamia to share gods or add foreign deities to an existing pantheon, but Jehovah reserved all divine powers to Himself. His terms were set out in the Bible:

'Thou shalt not bow down thyself (to any other gods), nor serve them: for I the Lord thy God am a jealous God, visiting the iniquity of the fathers upon the children unto the third and fourth generation of them that hate me'.[5]

Jehovah first manifested himself in around 2,000BC, when he told the childless Abraham of Ur that he would be the 'father of many nations'. Ironically for the son of Terah, an idol-maker in Ur, Abraham became the ancestor of the Jewish people, as well as the forerunner of Christianity and Islam. At Jehovah's command, Abraham, his wife Sarah and his household left Ur and embarked on a nomadic life that finally took them through Mesopotamia into present-day Israel and on to Egypt. Isaac, the son miraculously born to Abraham and his wife Sarah when he was 100 years old, and she was 90, became the subject of the most famous instance of sacrifice, or in this case, near-sacrifice, when God tested Abraham's faith. God commanded Abraham to sacrifice Isaac, and Abraham made preparations to do so. As the Book of Genesis records:

'. . . and Abraham built an altar . . . and laid the wood in order, and bound Isaac his son, and laid him on the altar upon the wood.'[6]

Abraham was about to light the fire for the burnt offering when, at the very last moment, a ram appeared with its horns caught in a thicket. The ram was sacrificed instead. This set the standard for

Eric & David Hosking

The sacrificial altar at Petra, Jordan. There appears to be a blood channel in the foreground of this partly natural stone structure. Hewn out of the local red sandstone, the ancient city of Petra became a stronghold of the Edomites and fell to the Romans in AD106.

sacrifices in ancient Judaism, which consisted of burnt animal offerings. The Israelites were, however, strongly warned against emulating their heathen neighbours in the practice of human sacrifice, or indeed, any other pagan rite. The punishments for contravening the divine command were awesome. The Bible contains a terrible warning of the punishment awaiting those Israelites who ignored the ban, took to human sacrifice and transferred their allegiance to Baal, a pagan deity worshipped throughout the Middle East.

'Because they have forsaken me, and have estranged this place, and have burned incense in it unto other gods . . . and have filled this place with the blood of innocents, they have built also the high places of Baal, to burn their sons with fire for burnt offerings unto Baal. . . . Therefore, behold, the days come, saith the Lord, that this place shall . . . be called . . . the valley of slaughter . . . and I will cause them to fall by the sword before their enemies . . . and their carcasses will I give to be meat for the fowls of the heaven, and for the beasts of the earth'.[7]

If prohibited forms of sacrifice were the subject of stringent rules, the permitted were just as strictly enforced. The basic practice, following the example of Isaac, Abraham's first and only son, was to sacrifice the first offspring of animals, whom God placed in a special class.[8] Only certain types of animal were eligible. They included young calves aged eight days to one year and cows or bulls aged up to three years. Lambs and young sheep aged eight days to one year, rams and ewes aged thirty-one days to two years, kids and young goats aged eight days to one year. Male and female goats aged two were also permitted. So were doves, either male or female, but only if the removal of a feather caused bleeding. Fully grown turtle-doves could be sacrificed, but they had to have large red and golden wings. These features showed that they were sufficiently mature.

All sacrifices had to be made in the proper manner, one that did not resemble mere slaughter or the practices of the pagans. The forbidden ways were carefully detailed:

'He that killeth an ox is as if he slew a man; he that sacrificeth a lamb, as if he cut off a dog's neck; he that offereth an oblation, as if he offered swine's blood; he that burneth incense, as if he blessed an idol. Yea, they have chosen their own ways, and their soul delighteth in their abominations.'[9]

References to the rules for the life to be lived in ancient Israel, including sacrificial practices, occur in many books of the Bible, but their main concentration is in the Book of Leviticus which lays down very specific instructions. Animals suitable for sacrifice, the manner of sacrifice and the use to which it must be put are all set down in the minutest detail:

'And the Lord called unto Moses, and spake unto him out of the tabernacle of the congregation, saying, speak unto the children of Israel, and say unto them, If any man of you bring an offering unto the LORD, ye shall bring your offering of the cattle, even of the herd, and of the flock. If his offering be a burnt sacrifice of the herd, let him offer a male without blemish: he shall offer it of his own voluntary will at the door of the tabernacle of the congregation before the Lord. And he shall put his hand upon the head of the burnt offering. . . . And he shall kill the bullock before the Lord: and the priests . . . shall bring the blood, and sprinkle the blood round about upon the altar that is by the door of the tabernacle of the congregation. And he shall flay the burnt offering, and cut it into pieces. And the sons of Aaron the priest shall put fire upon the altar, and lay the wood in order upon the fire. And the priests, Aaron's sons, shall lay the parts, the head, and the fat, in order upon the wood that is on the fire which is upon the altar: But his inwards and his legs shall he wash in water; and the priest shall burn all on the altar, to be a burnt sacrifice, an offering made by fire, of a sweet savour unto the Lord.'[10]

The instructions were the same for the sacrifice of sheep and goats. The proper way to sacrifice fowl – turtle-doves or young pigeons – was to wring off their heads and pluck away their crops and feathers before burning on the altar. The preparation of the sacrifices was also laid down. For instance, no meat offering could be made with honey or with yeast or other leavening material.

Most of the sacrifices to Jehovah were made for the welfare of the Jewish people and they were made three times a day. Sacrifices were also made on the Jewish festivals, such as Yom Kippur, the Day of Atonement, or Shavuot, the Festival of Weeks, which was a harvest festival. There were specific offerings, such as peace offerings, made in thanksgiving to God, or sin and guilt offerings made in atonement for wrongdoing. The scope of the sin offering was limited to lesser or uninentional crimes, such as ignorance of the Ten Commandments,

SAMUELE SACRIFICANTE PERDUNTUR HOSTES. Sam. Reg. 1. C. 7.

Samuel (bearded figure, right), last of the Old Testament judges who ruled ancient Israel, sacrifices a lamb as a burnt offering to Yahweh, the Hebrew sky god, in the face of his enemies, the Philistines. Print of unknown origin.

swearing, failure to tell the truth as a witness or touching any unclean animal or human. The more serious sins, such as blasphemy or open rebellion, could be dealt with only by the judgment of God.

Sacrifices were offered, too, for victory in battle, but here the Bible contains a cautionary tale. It concerns Jephthah, the Gileadite, who commanded the forces of Israel during their ongoing dispute with the Ammonites, another Semitic tribe. Ammonite resistance was such that in exchange for victory over them, Jephthah promised to sacrifice 'whatsoever cometh forth of the doors of my house to meet me, when I shall return in peace.'[11] God granted the victory, but on returning to his home in Mizpeh, Jephthah was met by his daughter, his only child. The promise to God had to be kept just the same, and Jephthah was obliged to make a burnt offering of this unfortunate young girl.[12]

Even though this event is probably apocryphal, it has been taken to indicate first of all how absolute promises to God had to be, and secondly, that such promises should not be lightly or carelessly made. This, in its turn, reflects the attitude to sacrifice in ancient Israel, which was hedged about with all sorts of disciplines and obligations. The priests who performed sacrifices had to fast first in order to purify themselves. Any deviation from any of the rules, however slight, was punishable, usually by death or ostracism.

An indication of what could happen when the rules were contravened was dramatically illustrated by the fate of Korah the Levite and his followers during the time when the Jews, led by Moses, were still wandering the Sinai Desert after their escape from Egypt. The Levites were religious functionaries of considerable importance. God had equated them with the firstborn, the most valued of the children of Israel.[13] Nevertheless, Korah was discontented at being ranked below the priests and maintained that Levites, too, should be allowed to perform priestly functions. Moses decided on a demonstration to prove that Jehovah's choice was not Korah, but Moses' brother Aaron, who had been divinely selected for the hereditary role of priest. Moses told Korah and each of his 250 followers to fill censers with incense, one of the offerings regularly made to Jehovah. The Bible describes how they paid the horrific consequences:

And Moses said, Hereby ye shall know that the LORD hath sent me to do all these works; for I have not done them of mine own mind. If these men die the common death of all men, or if they be visited after the visitation of all men; then the LORD hath not sent me. But if the LORD make . . . the earth open her mouth, and swallow them up, with all that appertain unto them, and they go down quick into the pit; then ye shall understand that these men have provoked the

LORD. And it came to pass, as he had made an end of speaking all these words, that the ground clave asunder that was under them: And the earth opened her mouth, and swallowed them up, and their houses, and all the men that appertained unto Korah, and all their goods. They, and all that appertained to them, went down alive into the pit, and the earth closed upon them: and they perished . . . And there came out a fire from the Lord, and consumed the two hundred and fifty men that offered incense.[14]

Sacrifices could be eaten after the ceremonies were performed. In general only parts of the animals, mainly the fats, were actually burned on the altar. In a thanksgiving celebration, part of the animal brought for sacrifice was consumed by the *kohanim*, the priests, and the rest was served at the celebratory meal. Sacrifice was also regarded as a strategy against the idol worship of the pagan faiths. The Jewish argument in favour of sacrifice was that it took away an animal's function as an object of worship. Being offered instead to God was much more appropriate.

However, the desirability of sacrifice was itself a matter of doubt in ancient Israel.[15] As the Book of Psalms puts it: '. . . thou delightest not in burnt offering. The sacrifices of God are a broken spirit: a broken and contrite heart'.[16]

This seems to suggest that the Jews were moving towards sacrifice, less as a physical act than as a spiritual metaphor for good behaviour or as a symbol to replace it. However, neither of these was the direct reason why sacrifices were later abandoned in ancient Israel. The explanation was much more commonplace, and much more painful. The sacrifices came to an end when the second temple was destroyed by the Romans in AD70, during the last great Jewish rebellion against their rule. Sacrifices had been reserved exclusively to the Temple and its priests, and could not be transferred to any other locale. Only a third Temple would do, but it was never built. Consequently, active sacrifice has never been restored in mainstream Judaism.

It survives among the Samaritans, however, a Jewish sect of very ancient origin, who make offerings of sheep as part of their annual

Passover rites; but otherwise in the Jewish world, sacrifice is strictly symbolic. At the Passover Seder, the meal commemorating the Biblical exodus of the Jews from Egypt, the 'paschal lamb' – the lamb sacrificed before they were able to depart – is represented by a roasted shank bone. In addition, Jews pray for the restoration of the Temple and, with that, the return of the sacrifices; but these prayers, too, are regarded as metaphors and serve only to record the allegiance of today's Jews to the ancient laws of their faith.

4

In Search of the Sun: Ancient Egypt

The life of Ancient Egypt depended on its agriculture, and agriculture depended on the River Nile and the fertile mud left behind after its annual floods receded. Beyond the Nile lay arid, barely habitable desert. Consequently, Egypt was regarded as 'the gift of the Nile', for without the river, the longest in Africa, there would have been no civilization. The Nile itself had many personifications, and friezes at the base of temple walls depicted them as figures passing in long processions loaded with gifts and offerings: produce from the fields or the mines or imports brought in by foreign trade.[1]

Festivals were the occasions for giving thanks to the gods for this inestimable bounty. This gratitude was expressed in a poem to Amon, king of the gods, in terms of offerings due to the: 'Lord of the Two Lands (of Upper and Lower Egypt), King of Eternity, lord of everlastingness, may they give you a thousand of bread, beer beef and fowl, a thousand of food offerings, a thousand of drink offerings . . .'.

The Festival of the Nile, held during the annual flooding of the river, was a lavish affair, in which statues of the gods were carried through the streets and offerings of food made at shrines. Most of these offerings were later eaten by the priests, but the general public got their share when the sacrifices of sheep, goats and cattle took place at the temple of the sun-god Ra in his capital of Heliopolis. The sacrifices were made at the foot of a tall, stone obelisk which Ra was thought to inhabit once the sun's rays touched the top. As well as the vast quantity of meat, bread, beer and cakes were distributed among the crowd of worshippers who had attended the sacrifices.[2]

37

Inside the Offertory chamber of
the tomb of Sety 1.

Egypt was so wonderfully blessed by Nature that there was little
need for ritual sacrifice in its more common form elsewhere – as an
attempt to divert the anger of the gods. The gods, quite obviously,
smiled on Egypt. Sacrifice, however, had another role to play apart from
thanksgiving, in the ceremonies and rituals connected with death.

It has often been said that the Ancient Egyptians were obsessed with
death. The building of a pharaoh's tomb usually began as soon as he
came to the throne and continued throughout his reign. The
monumental nature of the enterprise required many years to complete
and Day One of a new reign was not too early to start. However, there
were more than simply practical reasons behind the early preparation of
Ancient Egyptian tombs. In the ethos of Ancient Egypt, a
preoccupation with death was neither morbid nor fatalistic and death

was only the precursor to a new existence in another world. It would be truer to say, therefore, that if the Egyptians were obsessed, it was not with death, but with life. This was why their tombs were so lavishly equipped with everything the dead had enjoyed while they were still living: the tomb was simply another residence, and the afterlife was the place to continue earthly existence.

Egyptologists such as Flinders Petrie and Howard Carter, who discovered the tomb of the Pharaoh Tutankhamen in 1922, found stunning wealth in gold, silver, jewellery and other precious objects. These, naturally enough, captured excited headlines at the time and have done so ever since. However, Petrie, Carter and their fellow archaeologists were not treasure-hunters. They were scientists seeking the world of Ancient Egypt and using the tombs as a precious and unique resource. In 1880, Petrie pioneered a method of scientific record-keeping which archaeologists have used ever since. This made it possible to explore the fine detail of the tombs whose lesser, mundane contents were left behind when the grave-robbers of ancient and more recent times took away the more obvious riches. With this, a picture was gradually built up of the Ancient Egyptian way of life, their belief in reincarnation and the part sacrifices and offerings played in this process.

Egyptian belief in life after death – and death as a mirror image of life – was originally inspired by the myth of the saviour-god Osiris, who died and was later restored to life. The pharoahs were thought to be reincarnations of Osiris, and inherited from him the ability to live again after death. This same idea later spread among the general population of Egypt. They, too, sought new life beyond the tomb and from this arose the elaborate funerary rites, including mummification, offerings and sacrifices, all of which ensured continuance.

The task of reproducing earthly life in detail was a formidable one. The amount and value of the grave goods depended, of course, on the station an Egyptian had occupied in life. Artisans, for example, would be buried with tools, knives, scrapers, punches, grinders, awls and adzes. Graves also contained personal ornaments, jewellery, clothing,

Akhenaton makes an offering to Aton. In this monumental carving of *c.* 1350BC, the rays of the sun god bring fertility. The smaller figures bearing offerings are probably the Pharaoh's wife Nefertiti and one of their six daughters, one of whom married Tutankhamen. Akhenaton spent so much time on religious devotions that he lost a large part of the Egyptian empire.

even wigs and the supplies needed for hairdressing. The dead were equipped with writing materials, bottles of perfume or palettes for grinding the red ochre, antimony and other cosmetics. In this context, the detailed paintings found on the tomb walls were not meant simply for decoration. The tools and other items represented there were considered as good as, if not better than the original items: in the afterlife, the Egyptians believed, these objects would be magically transformed to their original state for the use of their owners. This was also believed to be true of the tiny models of tools which were buried with the dead.

These models served practical, as well as symbolic, purposes. First of all, they saved space, an important factor at a time when cemeteries had to contain numerous graves within the same confined area. Secondly, tools were valuable work items. Not every family could afford to 'lose' them, as it were, when their owner died. Third, and possibly most important, the cheaper representations were a safeguard against grave-robbing and therefore insurance against the dead being disturbed. In order to survive in the next world, they also needed food and this was part of the offerings placed in Ancient Egyptian tombs. The Papyrus of Ani, dated about 1240BC, better known as *The Book of the Dead*, set out specific instructions about the tasks to be done in preparing bodies for burial, the spells to be made to protect the deceased and a prayer for the provision of meat, milk and other foods:

'The Osiris Ani, whose word is truth, saith: Homage to thee, O Ra, the Lord of Truth, the Only One, the Lord of Eternity and Maker of Everlastingness. I have come before thee, O my Lord Ra. I would make to flourish the Seven Cows and their Bull. O ye who give cakes and ale to the Spirit-souls, grant ye that my soul may be with you'.

On the practical level, food was supposed to be provided regularly by the relatives and descendants of the dead. They left gifts of bread, beer and wine, beef, fowl, pomegranates or grapes together with flowers, textiles for making clothes and incense for making offerings. Here again, though, the Egyptians were pragmatic. As the generations went on, the dead could become distanced from the everyday life of their descendants. Even in their own generations, there could be circumstances – poverty and hardship, death or disability – which could bring family food offerings to an end. Provision was therefore made for these possibilities.

On most of the tombs, the wall paintings also depicted carved stone tables piled high with loaves of bread, cuts of beef, geese, lotus blossoms, fruits, vegetables, sweets and large vessels for wine and beer. Once again, in the afterlife, all these foods would be magically transformed and rendered edible once again.

The owner of the tomb, however, would not eat alone in the next life. The custom, already established in Mesopotamia, of burying servants, attendants and retainers in the same graves as their employers was also the custom in Egypt. On occasion, the numbers involved could be vast. King Wadji, a ruler of the First Dynasty of Ancient Egypt which came to power in about 3100BC, was buried with 335 members of his household. The bodies of 77 female and 41 male retainers shared the grave of Merneith, Wadji's queen. The definition of the retainer was not, however, confined to members of an immediate royal household. For instance, at the vast burial site at Saqqara, near Cairo, several craftsmen were buried close to some of the tombs, including an artist and a boat-builder.

In these mass burials, the servants and other attendants were placed in the same relative position they had occupied in life: their small graves were placed around the tombs of those they had served. Later, when the power of Egypt grew and the pharaoh became the focus of a huge centralized state, a royal tomb became a veritable complex including the graves of high officials, nobles and other leaders until a court of the dead was formed.[3] Within its parameters, all or any of these people could be restored to life and granted immortality by the powers of the pharaoh.

Presumably, though, these more exalted retainers died and were buried in their own good time. The path which servants took to death was different. Either they were buried alive, or they were poisoned and then buried. Archaeological evidence has revealed that not all live burials were voluntary, or if they were, then panic took over after these human sacrifices were sealed in the tomb and left there to suffocate as the air ran out. In some tombs, the positions of the bodies when found reveal that frantic attempts at escape were made.

All the same, in many of these multiple tombs, members of a royal household bore no sign of violence on their bodies and were not assaulted or executed before burial. It would seem to follow that they willingly accepted their fate, the inescapable fate of those who entered a Pharoah's service. The mindset of Ancient Egypt was such that this was accepted as a natural, if premature, end to Earthly life with the prospect, of course, that the afterlife awaited.

As time went on, however, there were practical reasons why men and women could no longer be used or at least used in great numbers, for symbolic ritual purposes: they were needed for life rather than death and the statuettes known as *shabtis*, also known as shawabtis and ushabtis, were buried in graves in their place. Shabti meant 'answer' or 'answerer' and first appeared in graves during the Eleventh Dynasty, which lasted from about 2025BC to 1979BC. They went on doing so for more than 1,700 years, until the practice died out in around AD395. The early shabtis were simple nude figures, wrapped in a 'shroud' made from linen and then placed in a miniature coffin. Later, during the reigns of pharaohs of the Middle Kingdom, between 1938BC and 1600BC, shabtis became more sophisticated and took the form of miniature mummies. These were often inscribed with the name and titles of their owner. It appears that however high-born an Egyptian was, even if he was the pharaoh himself, he was not excused his duties in the next world. This was the reason for the magic spell from Chapter 6 of the Book of the Dead which was inscribed on the shabtis. A space was left for the name of the deceased and the spell was meant to ensure that the shabti came to life at the appropriate time:

'O shabti, if name be summoned to do any work which has to be done in the realm of the dead to make arable the fields, to irrigate the land or to convey sand from east to west; 'Here am I,' you shall say, 'I shall do it'.

The first shabtis were inscribed with a prayer for offerings of food and were thought to house the *ka*, or soul, of the person buried in the tomb. The statuettes, between 10 cm and 23 cm high, were usually made of wood, stone, terracotta, or more commonly of faience, a paste made from pure ground quartz or quartz mixed with a small quantity of sand. Since Ancient Egypt was an agricultural society, many shabtis were made to resemble farm or field workers. To this end, they were produced carrying hoes to do this work in the afterlife. Some were also equipped with picks, bags of seed over the left shoulder and pots of water. Others were dressed as retainers and, as the production of these statuettes became more sophisticated during the Middle Kingdom after 2040BC, whole regiments of troops were produced, together with entire ships' crews, bakers, brewers, cooks and other craftsmen.

For centuries, minor officials in Egypt would be sacrificed and interred at the burial of the Pharaoh. Later, it became possible to escape this fate by substituting effigies made of wood (*shawabti*) or faience, known as *shabtis*. This one, dating from 600BC, is from the tomb of Hekemsaef.

Christies' Images

When shabtis were first introduced, there was normally only one to each grave; but, in time, very large numbers were buried in some of the more elaborate tombs. In the days of the New Kingdom, after about 1185BC, some 365 shabtis might be buried complete with 36 overseers equipped with whips to drive them to work and keep them at it until the work was done. The number 365 did not necessarily indicate one for every day of the year. Taharqa, the fourth king of the 25th Dynasty who reigned between 690 and 664BC, was buried with more than 1,000 shabtis, all carved from stone. Taharqa's shabtis were beautiful works of art, but there were also smaller, more humble statuettes which carried no inscriptions and had few recognizable human features. Sometimes, the faces and inscriptions were added in black ink after the shabti was made. The sale of shabtis ultimately grew into big business. They were sold over the counter, as it were, in the temples and were purchased by those who intended to have a life of leisure in the next world and leave all the work to the shabtis.

It was not only the people of Ancient Egypt who were reproduced in the form of shabtis. The sacred Apis bull was also buried with statuettes, representing bulls in miniature, and these served the dead animal in exactly the same way as their human counterparts. An Apis, which had to be black with a white diamond on its forehead, was

44

embalmed and buried after death with the same ceremony as the greatest pharaoh, and there was national mourning at its demise.

Although the bull was the most sacred among them, all animals were regarded as holy in Ancient Egypt. Each one was thought to be the incarnation on Earth of a god. Apis, for instance, was the manifestation of Ptah, the creator god of Memphis. All manner of other animals – baboons, dogs, cats, cows, hawks and ibises – were identified with their own gods and were treated in death with great ceremony and honour. At Saqqara, archaeologists found enormous numbers of animals, all mummified and placed in their own niches in underground galleries.[4] Saqqara was the venue for ordinary Egyptians who were not allowed to enter the temples except on festival days. Consequently, it became a place of pilgrimage and a ceremonial centre which pilgrims made long journeys to reach. They came to pray at the many shrines and temples, and make offerings to the gods in the form of a mummified animal which was placed in a pot and lodged in one of the many galleries. The choice of which animal to mummify belonged to the pilgrim, but otherwise the business of the animal cults at Saqqara was in the not always honest hands of the priests.

Hor, a priest and interpreter of dreams, who worked at Saqqara in the second century BC, left behind an archive which contains records of some very dubious practices. Pilgrims paid a fee for the pots that were supposed to contain the mummies of sacred birds. A serious scandal occurred when many of these pots were found to be empty, and a commission of enquiry charged six men with fraud and had them imprisoned. Afterwards, arrangements for the handling and burial of the sacred birds were radically overhauled.

Among the sacred birds, the ibis was probably the most popular focus of the animal cults in Ancient Egypt. They were reared in a lake close to Saqqara and, for as long as they lived, they lived in comfort. Like other animals, however, they became the subjects of what might be called 'sacrifice on demand'. When required and paid for by the pilgrims, the ibises were killed. Afterwards, they were sometimes mummified, sometimes dried out and covered in bitumen to preserve them. Either way, the highest standards of corpse preservation were rarely observed. After being wrapped in bandages, an ibis was placed in a pottery jar. Reflecting the popularity of the cult, as many as four million jars containing ibises may have been stacked in the underground galleries at Saqqara.

The Servants of the Ibis who performed this service at Saqqara were rather more honest than the Servants of the Hawk. Most of the ibis pots uncovered by archaeologists did, indeed, contain ibis mummies. However, hawks were not so easy to breed, and often had to be specially trapped. A single hawk, therefore, had to go a long way, and a large variety of fake contents were revealed in the so-called hawk pots. Instead of complete hawks, the pots could contain sticks, bones, parts of other birds or rodents and the mandibles of ibises which formed a frame filling out the bandaged mummy, but with nothing inside.[5]

Fraud among Eygptian priests was hardly surprising when the priesthood was often a part-time job. It generally lasted only three months before a priest returned to everyday life, which did not offer anything like the same opportunities for power and profiteering. In this situation, Ancient Egyptian priests were more like civil servants than religious leaders, even though they underwent a complex process of purification before entering the temple. However, their great influence as advisers, seers or interpreters of dreams far exceeded the powers of ordinary civil servants. Priests acted, too, as guardians of the gods in charge of providing them with offerings of food, clothes, metals, jewels, lamps, honey, grain, wine, oil and other crops. One of their duties was to burn incense to please the gods with its pleasant aroma.

If some of them were rogues, however, there was also a class of priests who were much more punctilious in their many functions. During his wide ranging travels in the fifth century BC, the Greek geographer and historian Herodotus observed the daily life and ritual of the priests and, among the many vivid descriptions contained in his *Histories*, outlined the great care taken to ensure that only the most suitable animals were selected for sacrifice. 'Male kine . . . are tested in the following manner', Herodotus wrote. 'One of the priests appointed for the purposes searches to see if there is a single black hair on the whole body, since in that case the best is unclean. He examines him all over, standing on his legs and again laid upon his back; after which he takes the tongue out of his mouth, to see if it be clean in respect of the prescribed marks . . . he also inspects the hairs of the tail to observe if they grow naturally.'

If the animal passed these stringent tests, the priests would twist 'a piece of papyrus round his horns, and attach thereto some sealing-clay, which he then stamps with his own signet ring. After this, the beast is led away; and it is forbidden, under penalty of death, to sacrifice an animal which has not been marked in this way.'[6]

When the time came for sacrifice, the animal was taken to an altar where a wood fire was lit and a libation of wine poured out. After the god was invoked, the animal was killed, its head cut off and its body flayed. According to Herodotus, an animal's head was treated as the fount of evil and was cursed by the priests. Afterwards, it was taken to the local market and sold to Greek traders. This might have been a reflection of the status of Greeks in Egypt in Herodotus's time. The Saite kings, who came to power in 664BC, had allowed foreigners of all kinds into Egypt – not economic migrants, as had once been the case, but foreigners with money, skills and commercial acumen.[7] The Greeks were the most active and enterprising of the foreigners. They came to monopolize Egyptian trade, which had once been a royal prerogative. Selling them the cursed and evil heads could therefore be interpreted as a form of passive resistance on the part of the priests.

However, if they found no Greek traders at the local market, the head was thrown in the river, with prayers that whatever evil might threaten Egypt or its people should be diverted on to it. Herodotus concluded that: 'These practices, the imprecations upon the heads and the libations of wine, prevail all over Egypt and extend to (sacrificial) victims of all sorts.'[8]

The method of sacrifice and the treatment afterwards varied from animal to animal. A steer sacrificed at a festival, for instance, was dismembered, and eviscerated. Its body was then filled with bread, honey, raisins, figs and aromatics like frankincense and myrrh. Oil was then poured over it, and it was burned. Meanwhile, those attending the ceremony fasted and, while the steer's body was being consumed by the fire, they flagellated themselves. That done, they sat down to a meal consisting of the other parts of the steer.

The head, being cursed and unclean, was never on the menu. Sheep could not be used either, leaving goats as the main sacrificial animal. It was forbidden to sacrifice a female, as they were sacred to the goddess Isis. Cows in particular were widely venerated in Egypt through their connection with Isis, a goddess whose image had the form of a woman, but with the horns of a cow on her head. According to Egyptian myth, Isis had once been the Greek goddess Io who was changed into a heifer by Zeus to protect her from the wrath of his wife, Minerva. Io, it appears, was flirting with Zeus when they were spotted by Minerva. Afterwards, the heifer was cruelly persecuted by Minerva and left Greece to wander the eastern Mediterranean until it reached Egypt. There, the heifer was miraculously restored to human form and, as Isis, was worshipped throughout Egypt even by those whose religious practices, sacrifices and deities were different from those of other Egyptians.[9]

5

A Classic Approach: Greece and Rome

All pagan faiths, including the religions of Ancient Greece and Rome, were marked by the omnipresence of the gods, who were thought to influence every conceivable aspect of human life. This concept was taken so far that divine presence permeated everyday life and no endeavour was thought to be valid without their sanction. There was no theology, as in monotheistic faiths, where belief centred on divinely ordained standards of human behaviour and obedience to God's commands. In paganism, it was the behaviour of the gods that counted and the gods were nothing if not volatile.

In ancient Greece, sacrifices to gain their favour were made on a daily basis. The gods of the Greek underworld received their offerings, of black animals, at an appropriately sombre time of day: after sundown. Sacrifices to other gods were made at dawn. Cows were offered to Hera, the mother of the gods, and heifers to Athena, goddess of war. Heifers were also sacrificed to Artemis, goddess of Nature, together with all manner of game. Demeter, goddess of corn, received offerings of pigs. Sacrifices to Poseidon, god of the sea, comprised horses; asses were offered to Priapus, god of fertility.

Whether or not the Greeks sacrificed humans in time of war or some great crisis such as an outbreak of plague has long been a matter for conjecture, but particular events in ancient Greek history would seem to confirm the practice. One of them was the custom of loading human scapegoats with collective sin and expelling them from Greek cities or killing them. Another was the execution of three Persian prisoners in

49

Ruggero Vanni

A relief from a Roman frieze depicting priests and a musician leading an elaborately dressed-up bull to the altar of Apollo, first century BC.

480BC before the decisive naval battle of Salamis, in which the Persian fleet was destroyed; and another, the killing of the men who assassinated King Philip II of Macedon in 336BC. Philip's son, Alexander the Great, ordered the assassins to be executed next to his father's tomb, in what looked more like an act of revenge, but revenge with sacrificial overtones.

In Ancient Greece, the sacrifice of bulls rather than humans was regarded as the highest and most noble offering of all. Bulls, sacrificed to Zeus, father of the gods and Dionysius, god of wine, were the epitome of strength, courage and aggression. They had an unusual reputation in ancient religion, far above that of any other animal. Sacrificing bulls, for example, was the central rite of Mithraism, a Persian faith which later gained numerous adherents in Rome in the second and third centuries AD. At around the same time, the taurobolium, the blood-offering of a bull, featured in Rome in the worship of Cybele, the Great Mother of the Gods.

The Greeks considered the sacrifice of a bull the best way of achieving a vital purpose: discovering the will of the gods through oracles and divination. The way in which the gods revealed their will was, however, indirect. It was 'read' in the rustling of the leaves of a sacred tree, movements of the water in a holy spring, or, more commonly, from the mouth of a priestess who went into a trance for the purpose. Whatever the method, the appropriate sacrifices had to be made first. The bull was, of course, the ideal, but the sacrificial animal was more commonly the less expensive and more numerous sheep. Some fifteen oracles have been located in Ancient Greece, including sites at Thebes, Corope in Thessaly, Delos, and Tyra. The oldest was said to be the oracle of Zeus at Dodona in the northwest. Undoubtedly the most famous, in fact world-famous, was the oracle of the god Apollo at Delphi, which was sited on Mount Parnassus not far from the Gulf of Corinth.

Anything and everything could be asked of an oracle – whether or not to marry, go on a journey, embark on a commercial enterprise, open a farm or found a new colony overseas. The oracle's answers were usually cryptic or ambiguous and might even take the form of riddles. Misunderstandings and misinterpretations were always possible. None of this, however, affected the Greeks' devotion to their oracles. The oracle at Delphi, for example, was in operation from around the fourteenth century BC, until early Christian times, a period of 1,500 or 1,600 years.

Individuals with a question to ask of the oracle offered a *pelanos*, or ritual cake, and provided the animal for sacrifice. A preliminary sacrifice was made outside the temple. The animal was led to the altar, usually in procession accompanied by music, and its head was sprinkled with water. If the animal tossed its head in response – a natural reaction – this was taken as the creature's 'assent' to its own death. The participants prayed to the god, and then threw the handsful of barley at the animal in a gesture that symbolized the act of violence that would follow. The grains were taken from a special basket which also contained the sacrificial knife.

Before sacrifice, this knife was used to cut hair from the animal's forehead. The hair was burned on the altar, as a foretaste of the full sacrifice. Most sacrificial animals had their throats cut, but in the case of larger, more powerful creatures, they were first stunned with an axe. The animal's blood flowed or was poured over the altar, eliciting a loud cry known as the *oloyge* from the women present. This was intended to announce the sacrifice to the gods or to express guilt and regret at the death of the animal. After this, a second sacrifice took place inside the temple. This took the form of placing all or part of the animal on a *trapeza*, or offering-table. That done, the priestess, known as the Pythia, suitably purified and crowned with laurel, went into her trance and pronounced the god's answer.

Once sacrificed, the animal was divided up for three purposes. The god's portion was set aside and wine was poured over it as it burned on the altar: typically, this consisted of the thigh bones covered in fat, with extra meat from the limbs. Priests usually supplemented this offering by placing some of the meat on a table in front of the god's statue or on its hands or knees. The participants in the sacrifice shared the entrails, which were roasted on skewers. The rest of the meat was boiled and usually taken home for consumption by the families of the participants or the public at large.[1]

The procedures of sacrifice in their form of strictly ordered ritual, were known as 'Olympian'. There were, however, several variants. One of them concerned sacrifices of animals to the gods of the underworld and to the Greek heroes. The meat of these sacrifices was not consumed, and before the animals were killed, their heads were not held upwards, with the throat exposed. Instead, they were pushed down into a pit or a hearth and then dispatched. Wine was not used for libations.

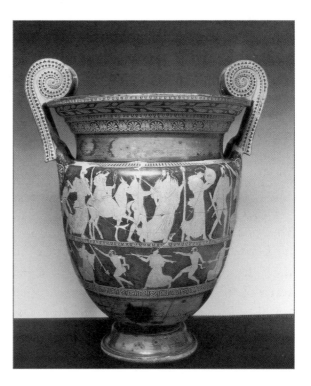

Greek krater vase depicting a procession to a sacrifice to the sun god, Apollo. (Archivo Iconografico SA)

Other variations occurred when a sacrifice was made to confirm an oath or contract: the meat was not eaten and the carcass was disposed of by throwing it into the sea. A curious procedure accompanied the sacrifice of an ox at the Bouphonia, which took place during the festival of Dipolieia in Attica, east-central Greece. This was a very ancient festival, dating from the thirteenth century BC and involved a trial to decide who, or what, was responsible for killing the sacrifice. It had become something of a charade. The culprit was always the sacrificial knife or axe with which the deed had been performed. This, though, effectively shifted the blame from any human agent involved.

The comparatively decorous method of Olympian sacrifice had its complete opposite in the rites performed at Patrae in honour of the goddess Artemis. The method of sacrifice was the 'holocaust'. First, green logs of wood were stacked around the altar and a fire was lit.

Pausanius, a Greek writer of the second century BC, in his *Description of Greece*, outlined what happened next:

'They throw animals onto the altar, including edible birds . . . wild boar, deer and gazelles, and some bring wolf and bear cubs, others fully grown animals. . . . I saw there a bear and other beasts that had been thrown on, struggling to escape the first rush of the flames and escaping by brute force, but those who threw them on put them back on the fire . . .'.[2]

Pausanias claimed that he could not 'recall anyone being harmed by the wild beasts', but the obvious danger involved in sacrificing live animals, whether wild or domesticated, may explain why this type of offering was comparatively rare in Ancient Greece, where no major festival was without its sacrifices. The most sacred festival of all was the Eleusinian Mysteries held every year at the city of Eleusius, some 22 km west of Athens. The Mysteries, which took their name from the Greek *musterion*, meaning secret, were performed in the Greek month of Boedromion – late September and early October – in honour of Demeter and Persephone, Demeter's daughter by Zeus. The proceedings opened when the participants – who had to be Greek citizens of impeccable character – walked into the sea carrying a piglet for sacrifice. Towards the end of the proceedings, which were guarded by an oath of secrecy required of all participants, libations of a sacred liquid were poured on the ground.

Worshippers came from all over Greece to attend the Mysteries; and, because this was a very volatile area, always subject to warfare between rival city-states, a 55-day truce was declared to enable them to travel to and from the festival, which lasted nine days. A similar truce was in operation for the sacred games held on Mount Olympus every four years in honour of Zeus. The Games lasted five days, and all participants, judges, scrutineers and representatives of the various Greek cities attended the sacrifice of one hundred bulls which occurred on the morning of the third day.

The focus of sacrifice at Mount Olympus was the great altar to Zeus, which stood at the spot where, according to legend, the god threw a

Previous page: The fabulous burial of the Lord of Sipan, Peru, *c.* AD200. A ruler of the Chimu culture, the 'Lord' is named after the place in the Lambayeque Valley where he was found in 1987, buried with his wife, retainers and elaborate grave goods. Little is known about him. The picture is of a reconstruction in the national museum at Lima. (*Kevin Schafer*)

Left: Inca child. Unblemished maidens from upper-class families were offered at the ceremony of Capacocha. Taken to meet the Sapa Inca, they were given a public feast then walled-up alive in mountain caves. Sacrifices followed important events such as earthquakes or the death of an emperor and brought high honour on the families. The immuring of children is also common in Germanic tribal lore. (*Charles & Josette Lenars*)

Below, left: An Aztec sacrificial brazier used for burnt offerings, found at Teotihuacan, Mexico. (*Gianni Dalli Orti*)

Below: Chavin mummy, from Peru. Unlike the Egyptians, whose mummification practices were scientific, corpses in ancient Peruvian Indian cultures were preserved by exposure to the dessicating winds of the high plains and thus, offered to the sky gods. The massive hole in the skull suggests a violent cause of death. (*Galen Rowell*)

The stepped pyramid at Chichen Itza. There are conflicting theories as to why the Maya practised human sacrifice on such a scale. The rites accompanying the sacrifices were devoted to the sun god and may have been connected with the ending of a 'world cycle' predicted by their sophisticated calendar. (*The Purcell Team*)

An Aztec illustration, depicting a sacrifice in preparation. The eagle is reminiscent of the stoneware 'heart-basin' shown on page 85. By divine direction, the Aztecs founded their capital at Tenochtitlan, the 'place of the prickly pear', hence the cactus plant in the foreground. (*Gianni Dalli Orti*)

The astounding spectacle of a 'sacrifice' to the sun god, Viracocha, takes place every 24 June at the New Year festival of Inti-Raymi at Cuzco, Peru. 'Priests' bear the shining solar disc around the arena, while behind them follows a procession of mummified corpses dressed in red robes. The highlight of the ceremony is when the 'Sapa Inca' elected for the year gives the oration in Quechua, the ancient language of the Inca. (*Ric Ergenbright*)

The Pyramid of Kukulkan, the 'feathered serpent', Chichen Itza. The remains of the temple complex can be seen in the foreground. Though monumental and astonishingly well crafted by master-masons, Toltec-Maya pyramids were never on the same scale as the Great Pyramid in Egypt. As a clue to its ritual purpose, Kukulkan has 364 flanking steps, plus a common top step, making one step for each day of the solar year. (*Michael T. Sedam*)

Aztec mask. The 'nose' of the skull is the protruding blade of a sacrificial knife. It is claimed that upper-class Aztecs wore the cured skins of sacrificial victims as costumes at drunken orgies, although other authorities state that a strict moral code was enforced. (*Gianni Dalli Orti*)

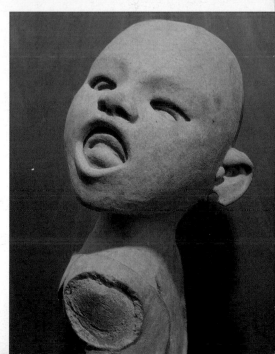

One of the most terrifying objects of human sacrifice was Xipe Totec, the childlike 'Flayed Lord' of the Aztecs. He is depicted within the skin of a screaming victim. Modern sources have suggested that Aztec rites masked State-sponsored cannibalism on an industrial scale (e.g. Harner, 1977). (*Werner Forman*)

Above: This pathetic row of jars visible in the ruins of the Temple of Baal at Thuburbo Major near Carthage contains the burnt remains of children believed to have been sacrificed about 500BC. An altar to sacrificed children is nearby. (*Charles & Josette Lenars*)

Below: An Egyptian offering-bearer. The 'sacrifice' is possibly a stylised pomegranate. Young Egyptian males were conscripted into the priesthood but served for only a few months at a time. (*Archivo Iconografico SA*)

Above: The Temple of Baal near Carthage, in modern-day Tunisia. Reports of the live immolation of children in the 'holocaust' may have been exaggerated by Roman chroniclers, but the Carthaginians certainly resorted to mass sacrifice in times of trouble. (*Ruggero Vanni*)

Above: Among the richest find of grave goods in history, in 1922 the tomb of Tutankhamen produced this elaborately gilded and decorated throne, on which the boy Pharaoh is seen basking in the rays of Aton, the sun god. Offerings are being made to him by his wife, one of the daughters of the sun-worshipping Pharaoh, Akhenaton. (*Michael Nicholson*)

Above: Egyptian morticians are mummifying a bull in this mural from Saqqarah, near Memphis, *c.* 2600BC. Animals with appropriate markings were consecrated to Apis, the bull-god, on his birthday. Drowned in the Nile, their mummies were ceremonially entombed in the Sarapaeum. (*Gian Berto Vanni*)

Right: *The deceased making an offering to Horus*. Illustration from the Egyptian Book of the Dead. Copies of the book and other instructions for achieving a successful transition to the afterlife were interred with the deceased. (*Gianni Dalli Orti*)

The largest sacrificial object yet discovered, the restored 'solar boat' of Cheops (Khufu) has pride of place in its own museum beside the Great Pyramid at Gizeh, Egypt. The Pharaoh was entombed in about 2550BC with not one, but *five* of these 140 ft seagoing barges, found in shallow stone pits during excavations in the 1950s. The sacrifice had been intended to row the Pharaoh through the sky to meet/become the sun god. The tiny figure standing on the gallery (right) gives scale to this astonishing find. (*Wolfgang Kaehler*)

thunderbolt and so marked the place as his own. The vast extent of the burnt offerings made there was discovered when archaeologists began to excavate the ancient grove, the Altis, which was the main focus of the site. Excavations began in the eighteenth century, and eventually reached the altar, which was found buried deep inside a mound of ash.[3]

When neither the Games nor the Eleusinian Mysteries were taking place, it was, of course, open season for war in Ancient Greece. Sacrifices had their part to play as offerings designed to induce the gods to grant victory, and armies marching to war used to take flocks of sheep and goats with them for the purpose. Active military life was regularly punctuated by sacrifices as the blessing of the gods was sought for every move an army might make. This included crossing the borders between the city-states, building a camp, attacking a town or deciding on a line of advance. The final scene of sacrifice was the battlefield itself and there could be no fighting before the sacrifice was made. In 479BC, when the city-states of Athens, Tegea and Sparta confronted the invading Persians at the battle of Plataea, the Spartan troops delayed their advance until the proper sacrifices had been offered to the gods.[4] The Persians had no such qualms and poured arrows down on the static line of Spartans, killing many of them. Fortunately, this had no effect on the outcome of the battle, which saw the Persians decisively defeated.

After victory in battle, it was customary for the Greeks to make a sacrifice of the enemy's arms and armour to the god they considered responsible for their triumph. Some victories were more significant than others, and where the survival of Greece itself had been under threat – as it was during the Persian invasions – a large-scale festival, the Soteria, from the Greek for 'deliverance', would be held as a thanksgiving. Sixteen known Soteria were held, accompanied by appropriate sacrifices, with Delphi as the scene of the best known. This Soteria took place after the Celts, who were threatening to invade and conquer Greece, were defeated at Thermopylae in 278BC.

By that time, the beliefs of Ancient Greece had already permeated Rome and Italy. In legend, the Greek gods were said to have been

Wolfgang Kaehler

The Tholos in the Sanctuary of Athena, Delphi, Greece. The famous 'oracle' on Mount Parnassus was a Pythian woman whose prophetic utterances were interpreted by priests, about 590BC. Sacrifices of boars and bulls were made in payment at the Temple of Apollo. Delphi soon became a popular commercial centre, with an annual festival and games.

56

brought to Rome by Aeneas, who fled to Italy after the destruction of Troy, which ended the bitter, ten-year Trojan War. A rather more likely explanation, however, lies in the hellenization of Italy, which was so intensively colonized by Greeks that it was termed *Magna Graecia*, Greater Greece. Another source of Roman religion, which had itself absorbed Greek influences, was the faith of the Etruscans in Etruria, in northern Italy. The Romans looked on the ancient, highly cultured Etruscans as their mentors, and absorbed many Etruscan concepts into their own faith. One was the principle of *manus*, the great driving force behind all spiritual life which, for the convenience of humans, took the form of the gods. A further inheritance from the Etruscans was human sacrifice, as performed in 228BC when Rome was in dire peril from their longstanding, and savage, enemies, the Celtic Gauls. The Gauls had settled in northern Italy and the Romans were so panicked by the threat they posed that the senate ordered the live burial of two Gauls and two Greeks in the Forum Boarium. This ritual was repeated in 216BC, after the crushing Roman defeat at Cannae during the Second Punic War against the Carthaginians, and again in 114BC, when the power of the senate was in danger from the military dictator Gaius Marius. The senate apparently took their cue from the Sybilline Books of prophecy kept in the Temple of Jupiter. However, Polybius, the Greek historian of Rome's rise to international power, had his own more worldly explanation.

'There is utmost excitement and fear in the city. . . . All the oracles that had ever been delivered to the Romans were in men's mouths, every temple and every house was full of signs and prodigies, so that vows, sacrifices, supplicatory processions and litanies pervaded the town. For, in season of danger, the Romans are much given to propitiating both gods and men, and there is nothing at such times in rites of the kind that they regard as unbecoming or beneath their dignity.'

A further import from Etruria, the gladiatorial games, best known as a bloody and popular sport in the arenas of imperial Rome, had their origins in Etruscan religious belief. Though sport in general was

Mimmo Jodice

The Sacrifice of Iphiginea. Agamemnon offers his daughter to appease the goddess Artemis in this colourful mural found at Pompeii. Sacrifice was a popular theme in Roman art, as were Greek myths. In some versions Artemis took pity on Iphigenea and substituted a deer.

intimately tied up with blood sacrifice in both Ancient Greece and Ancient Rome, these games initially had nothing to do with public entertainment. They were part of the rituals, first recorded in Rome in 264BC, that accompanied the funeral of Junius Pera, a member of the prestigious Brutus family. On that occasion, three pairs of swordsmen fought each other to the death, presumably for the honour of giving the dead man an armed guard in the next world.

Like the Greeks, the Romans offered domestic animals on their altars, reserved special portions for the god to whom the sacrifice was made and then proceeded with a sacrificial banquet. The fitness of the sacrifice was of special concern. Once the animal had been killed, its vital organs – liver, gall bladder, intestines, lungs and heart – were examined to make sure they were healthy and therefore acceptable to the god. If not, then another animal was sacrificed and examined and none was offered to the god until the *popae*, or sacrificers, were satisfied. Procedure differed according to the location of the god in question. Sacrifices to the celestial gods were burned on the altar. Offerings to sea deities, like Neptune, god of the sea, were thrown into the water. Gods of the underworld received their offerings in pits or on the ground.

In Rome, the sacrificial banquet could take several forms. Sometimes, it was confined to those who had been present at the sacrifice; sometimes the meat was served at vast communal banquets, or it was sold in butchers' shops so that all could buy it and benefit at one remove from the offering made. Etruscan practice was involved in this context: as in Etruria, the livers and entrails of sacrificed animals were used in Rome to divine future events. However, to complicate the picture, various cults had their own practices: in the worship of Attis and Cybele, Great Mother of the Gods, the blood of the sacrificed bull rather than its meat was central to the sacrifice, and in the cult of Hercules, the meat had to be eaten or burned before nightfall.[5]

Public worship in Rome was reflected in the home, where the paterfamilias, the all-powerful head of the family, made sacrifices, directed prayers and called on the help of dead ancestors in time of trouble. The *lares* and *penates*, the protectors of the family, had their special shrine in every home where sacrifices were offered, and at every meal, as in the temples, the gods were given their share of the food. The paterfamilias exercised total dominance over all members of his household and, theoretically, his power was the power of life and death. This was typical of the deeply conservative society of Rome in which

From the Temple of Vespasian at Pompeii, another bas-relief of a Roman bull sacrifice, possibly for the purpose of divination. The wealthy woman in the foreground may have paid for the ceremony to be held.

males were dominant and among other aspects of life, monopolized most religious observance and ritual. This diverged from Greek practice, in which there were both male and female priests, each serving deities of their own sex. Each was attached to their own cults, temples or to special festivals. They were essentially part-timers, performing their religious duties when required, but otherwise leading normal 'secular' lives.

In Rome, the priests belonged to colleges or brotherhoods which had their own specialities. The most important were the *pontifices*, headed by the Pontifex Maximus, who advised on religious law. The Fratres Arvales, or Arval Brothers, formed a college of great antiquity and concentrated on offering yearly public sacrifices for the fertility of the fields. The *epulones* supervised religious banquets and the *augures* were in charge of divination.

Of these duties, augury was by far the most taxing. The Greeks were anxious enough to discover the will of the gods, but with the Romans, it verged on an obsession. It was not simply a matter of receiving the divine decision and accepting it. Tremendous efforts were made by Roman augurers to secure a favourable answer. Several successive sacrifices were made – up to thirty or more – in order to overturn negative readings, clarify those that were ambivalent or simply to make absolutely sure that the gods meant to favour an enterprise they had already approved.

There was, too, the suspicion that the sacrifices might not have been exact in every detail, so causing the auspices to be unfavourable. There was much to be considered: sacrifices had to be performed in the correct manner by the right person and take place at the right time in the right place. In a majority of cases, the right place was Rome itself. Sacrifices and the taking of auspices that were traditionally sited there were illegal anywhere else. Even within Rome, locations for sacrifice were very specific and the devotion of the bureaucratic Romans to proper procedure was such that on one occasion, a young man risked his life to perform his duties.

In 390BC, when the Celtic Gauls attacked and occupied Rome, the time arrived for sacrifices to be offered for an annual festival. These sacrifices were the monopoly of the family of Fabius and the place to offer them was on the Quirinal hill. At this time, the Gauls were besieging the Capitol and among the Romans inside was one Caius Fabius Dursuo. He was the right man in the wrong place. Caius therefore left the Capitol and proceeded through the enemy lines, taking the sacred vessels with him, until he reached the Quirinal. Having performed his duties, he returned to the Capitol. Fortunately, the Gauls appear to have been sufficiently impressed by his courage and piety that they made no move to molest him.

The complete opposite of Caius' devotion was the behaviour of Gaius Flaminius, general and political maverick. During the Second Punic

War with Carthage, Flaminius was deprived of his consulship after the auspices that had been in favour of his election were cancelled. This cancellation could have been a political move by Flaminius' many enemies, for he was a notorious opponent of senatorial power in Rome. It was therefore very much in character when the enraged Flaminius left Rome for his military camp, conducted his own auspices, found them favourable – of course – and assumed the consulship on his own account. In Rome, this was tantamount to blasphemy. Not long afterwards, in 217BC, Flaminius was ambushed and killed by the renowned Carthaginian general Hannibal at Lake Trasimenus, in central Italy. His defeat and death were afterwards ascribed, not to a lack of military expertise, but to the illegality of his sacrifices and augury.

Locations for sacrifice and worship existed outside Rome, of course, but this was simply another side of the same strict rule. The rule revolved around the choice of the gods and their choice was incontrovertible. They had decreed, for instance, that the Feriae Latinae, the Festival of Jupiter Latiaris, should be held on Mons Cavo in the Alban Hills near Rome. Here, the two newly elected consuls offered a libation of milk and a white, never-yoked heifer was sacrificed. Likewise, Mount Soracte in southern Etruria was the only place for women to offer sacrifices to Feronia, the Etruscan goddess of fire and fertility.

The connection between women and a fertility goddess was obvious, but in general, the religious role of Roman women was very limited. In keeping with the male-dominated ethos of Ancient Rome, women were not counted among those in authority who had the right to make communal sacrifices. Probably their most important religious role was as Vestal Virgins, tending the Temple of Vesta, goddess of the hearth. There were six Vestal Virgins at any one time, and to be fit for this important role, they had to give at least thirty celibate years to their deity. The punishment for breaking their vows of chastity was live burial. Vestal Virgins were chosen as early as age six by the Pontifex Maximus, the high priest, and normally came from aristocratic families. Because of their special status, the Virgins were freed from the dominance of their paterfamilias. The Virgins' task was to tend the sacred temple fire, fetch water from a sacred spring, prepare the ritual food for the goddess and offer sacrifices. It was their responsibility to mix the *mola salsa*, the grain and salt used in the public sacrifices offered at the festival of Vestalia, in June, where they officiated.

After their thirty-year service was over, Vestal Virgins were permitted to marry, but very few did so, since this was considered unlucky. By contrast, the priestesses known as *flaminicae* acquired their position through marriage. A *flamina* was the wife of one of the *flamines*, the fifteen priests whose task was give exclusive service to a particular deity. The *flamen*, whose name meant 'he who burns offerings', made daily sacrifices, assisted by his wife. However, if she died, he was no longer eligible to serve his deity.

Surprisingly perhaps, for a people so devoted to tradition and so obsessively perfectionist in their own faith, the Romans were generally tolerant of other religions. One of the most widespread and influential was Mithraism, a sun-god cult especially popular among Roman soldiers. Several cults flourished within the Empire, including the worship of Apollo, Bacchus, Ceres and other individual gods and goddesses. Egyptian imports centred around Osiris and Serapis. One of the more curious cults, the cult of Terminus, centred worship on a boundary stone which was garlanded with flowers and received sacrifices of lambs or pigs. Death or, later, a heavy fine, was the punishment for moving the stone.

However, the religion the Romans refused to tolerate and one of the few they actively persecuted, was the faith that finally superseded their own: Christianity, which excluded obligatory worship of the 'divine' Roman Emperors and the rituals associated with them. Christianity, adopted throughout the Roman Empire after AD313, brought with it a new concept of sacrifice. In Christianity, sacrifice became symbolic rather than actual, a matter of spiritual discipline rather than physical oblation. For Christians, Christ on the Cross had been the last blood sacrifice and the one that stood for all time. It was a unique and, for the Romans, a very dangerous idea.

6

Twilight of the Gods: Northern Europe

The advent of Christianity in the Roman Empire meant neither the demise of paganism, nor of its rituals and sacrifices. The struggle to overcome its age-old power and the hold it exercised in Europe would take many centuries. All Europe did not become officially Christian until after 1386. Even then, pockets of paganism persisted and instances of the old practices were still occurring as late as the nineteenth century.

Constantine I, the first Christian emperor, failed in his attempt to ban the gladiatorial games in AD325 and his successors went on failing for another two centuries. Like most ancient sports, the games were intimately connected with blood sacrifice. For instance, participants at sports meetings practised a rite of 'blooding', by sitting in a pit while the blood of a sacrificed bull washed over them from above. In Rome, an annual sacrifice took place after a two-horse chariot race. One of the winning horses was killed with a spear. His tail was cut off and taken to the temple, where the blood was allowed to drip onto a hearth. The resultant paste of blood and ashes was preserved, together with the rest of the horse's blood. The horse's severed head was displayed in public.

Constantine was no more successful in AD353, when he banned all pagan sacrifices and the temple rituals that went with them. This edict threatened the customs long observed at all the sports festivals throughout the empire, including the most prestigious of all, the games celebrated every four years on Mount Olympus in Greece. Emperor Theodosius II, who conducted a vigorous anti-pagan campaign after AD379, forbade all sacrifices in AD391 and all attendance at the temples where they took place. The following year, he went further and prohibited all worship of pagan gods. In AD393, he put an end to the games at Mount Olympus. Theodosius was a thoroughly despotic ruler, but even he was unable to expunge paganism from his empire. The games and the athletic festivals and the blood cults carried on as before. His grandson, Theodosius II, took even more drastic action. In AD426, he ordered all pagan temples razed to the ground, including the temple of Zeus at Olympia, which was afterwards left with only its bare foundations.

Even this did not achieve the desired Christian objective. The traditional sites might be gone, but the sports simply took their pagan sacrifices and their rituals elsewhere. The famed Olympic Games transferred to the Phrygian city of Antiochia, in present day Turkey and, with their sacrifices, proved so popular that finally, in AD520, the ultimate threat was issued by Emperor Justin I: the Games were not only prohibited, but anyone contravening the ban would be subject to the death penalty. Then, and only then, did the message at last get through.

This was as much a triumph for the Judaeo-Christian principle of the sanctity of life as it was for the Emperor. The principle, which became fundamental in Christian doctrine, had been outlined four centuries before Justin's final success by the Christian theologian and moralist Tertullian. He wrote in his *De Spectaculis* ('On the Games'): 'Temples or tombs, we abominate both kinds of idolatry. We know neither sort of altar, we adore neither sort of image; we pay no sacrifice . . . and we do not eat of what is offered in sacrificial or funeral rite.'[1]

There was, however, more to the pagan practices of Europe than those of the Greeks and the Romans in the time before the empire turned Christian.

The Celts, who occupied vast areas across Europe before their conquest by Rome, the German tribes along the Rhine border with Rome and, further away from Roman influence, the Scandinavian Vikings, the peoples of the Baltic, eastern Europe and Russia, all had

Jan Butschofsky-Houser

Newgrange, Valley of the Boyne, N. Ireland. This and lesser chambered 'tombs' are a mystery as few human remains have ever been found inside what were previously thought to have been neolithic burial sites. With its solar alignment on the winter solstice and recently-discovered Venus 'observatory', Newgrange may have hosted fertility rites involving sacrifice.

their own rituals, customs, deities, mythologies and other apparatus of pagan belief.

The Celts had a particularly fearsome reputation that derived mainly from Roman dread of their savagery in war and the air of mystery and sorcery that surrounded their priests, the Druids. Fear and superstition gained such a hold on the minds of the Roman legions before the invasion of Britain ordered by the Emperor Claudius in AD43 that they mutinied and refused to leave the shores of France. To them, Britain was beyond the limits of the known world. It was a strange, magical place called Isola Sacra, the Sacred Isle. On this isle, the soldiers believed, there were groves and forests where supernatural spirits lived. The Druids, they considered, were wizards who cast spells and practised sorcery and magic. They performed horrible rituals and sacrificed humans and animals to their gods. Afterwards, their altars, the dolmens, were said to be drenched in blood.

However, the Roman Army was not the best in the ancient world for nothing. Britain was duly invaded and afterwards conquered; the Romans sparing no effort in their persecution of the Druids. All the same, the Roman image of the Druids was not all fearful fancy and imagination. Druid power in Celtic society was all-encompassing. They were lawyers, judges, doctors and advisers to the Celtic kings as well as religious leaders and prophets. Just how important the Druids were was expressed in the *Texts of the Tain*, a great book of Irish myths, which states: 'The men of Ulster must not speak before the king, the king must not speak before his Druid'.

The Celts believed their gods were everywhere – in streams, wells, mountains, rivers or forests – and sacrifices were such a vital part of Celtic life that a disobedient or recalcitrant tribe was punished by being banned from attending the ceremonies. These ceremonies were conducted by the Druids in sacred oak groves possessing a supernatural terror so all-pervasive that the Celts themselves feared to venture there. In his *Pharsalia*, the Roman poet Lucan wrote of just such a grove in southern France:

'A grove there was untouched by men's hands from ancient times, whose interlacing boughs enclosed a space of darkness and cold shade, and banished the sunlight from above. . . . Gods were worshipped there with savage rites, the altars were heaped with hideous offerings and every tree was sprinkled with human gore. . . . The people never resorted thither to worship at close quarters, but left the place to the gods for, when the sun is in mid-heaven or dark night fills the sky, the priest himself dreads their approach and fears to surprise the lord of the grove.'[2]

The material of Celtic offerings to their gods was little different from the Roman. They, too, sacrificed sheep, goats and bulls. Like the

Romans, too, they used sacrifice for the purposes of divination. This, it appears, involved human sacrifice,[3] a controversial subject in connection with Celtic life. The original information relies mainly on observations made in the second and first centuries BC by the Greek Stoic philosopher Poseidonius, who was considered the most learned man of his time. Later, the writings of Poseidonius were used by other travellers and historians such as Strabo and Diodorus Siculus, both of them Greeks. Their picture of the Celts – Diodorus wrote: 'Their aspect is terrifying' – could have been useful for Roman propaganda which had an interest in labelling them as savage barbarians.[4]

Whether or not the tales of Celtic human sacrifice were accurate, the ancient descriptions were certainly graphic. For example, in his *Histories*, Strabo, writing in the first century BC, described how humans were killed for divination:

'They devote to death a human being and stab him with a dagger in the region of the diaphragm and when he has fallen, they foretell the future from his fall and from the convulsions of his limbs and moreover, from the spurting of the blood, placing their trust in some ancient and long continued observation of these practices.'[5]

Among the Celtic Gauls, the method of killing seems to have varied with the god concerned. Lucan recorded how sacrifices to Taranis, who was probably a Celtic sky god, were burned. For offering to Teutates, the protector god, sacrifices were drowned, or they were hanged in the case of Esus, god of the arts.[6]

Strabo described further ways of killing 'victims' and also gave details of Celtic sacrifice by holocaust:

'They used to strike a human being . . . in the back with a sword. . . . They would shoot victims to death with arrows or impale them in the temples or having devised a colossus of straw and wood, thrown into the colossus cattle and wild animals of all sorts and humans, and then make a burnt-offering of the whole thing.'

Celtic offerings of humans in holocaust sacrifices do not appear to have been confined to the spectacular burning of the 'Wicker Man'. Archaeological excavations at the Celtic hill fort at Danebury in

Michael St Maur Sheil

Neolithic settlers in north-west Europe also raised platforms to the sky, *c.* 3,500BC. This dolmen and altarstone at Poulnabrone in County Clare are in an area containing over 70 megaliths, known as the Burren. Bones belonging to 22 adults and six children were found beneath it.

southern Britain revealed the wholesale burial of human and animal sacrifices in the pits where grain was stored. Once empty, these pits were filled with complete corpses, parts of corpses, including heads – a particular focus of Celtic worship – complete or part-animals such as sheep, cattle, pigs, horses, dogs and ravens, as well as tools, bridles, saddles, grain and the quernstones on which it was ground.

One of the bodies was found buried under a pile of large rocks. Possibly, he had been stoned to death. The contents of the pit have been interpreted either as thank-offerings to the underground gods for preserving the grain in the pits or as propitiation in hopes of a good harvest.[7] Another body discovered by archaeologists, this time in a peat bog in Lindow, Cheshire also bore the marks of placatory sacrifice in the triple form that had magical significance for the Celts. He had been hit on the head and then strangled, after which his throat was cut. Lindow Man, remarkably preserved by the peat in which he was buried, probably died sometime in the first or second century AD.

As in the Celtic religion, the sacred grove was the focal point of German pagan faith and served a similar purpose in the Baltic lands, Scandinavia and Russia. The Germans had a spiritual attitude towards these places and also considered temples and their idols unseemly in relation to their gods. In AD98, in his *Germania*, the Roman historian Tacitus wrote:

'In general, they judge it not to be in keeping with the majesty of heavenly beings to confine them within walls or portray them in any human likeness. They consecrate woods and groves and they apply the names of gods to that mysterious presence which they see only with the eye of devotion.'[8]

Despite this mystical concept, the spilling of blood was still common in Germanic religious practices. Tacitus found that the tribe of Semnones who lived in the region of present day Brandenburg, near Berlin, sacrificed a human before commencing their religious rituals. The Hermiundurii sacrificed their defeated enemies. The Germanic way of offering to their gods the belongings, equipment and persons of those they conquered involved total destruction. In the fourth of his *Seven Books of History Against the Pagans*, written three centuries after the event, the Spanish Christian writer Paulus Orosius described what happened after the Germanic Cimbri captured two military camps in the lower valley of the River Rhine in 105BC:

'Garments were torn apart and thrown away, gold and silver hurled into the river, the soldiers' armour was chopped in pieces, the horses' harness destroyed, the horses themselves thrown in the river and the men hanged from trees. . .'[9]

Sacrifice in the Germanic world was closely linked to the Nordic, where cairns, each with a name commemorating the event, were erected at the places where blood sacrifices had been celebrated. Scandinavians seem to have differed from the Germans in their ideas about suitable sites for worship and the representation of deities by means of images. Although much of their worship took place in the open air or in sacred groves, they also built temples, usually in the form of wooden buildings, or in Viking Iceland, structures resembling farmhouses. Inside, there were chancels containing altars ringed by images of the gods. These altars were equipped with a sacrificial bowl used by priests to offer sacrifices to the gods. The nature of the sacrifices was evident in the blood-sprinkler attached to the bowl.[10]

The Nordic sagas serve as the source of many details of Scandinavian paganism, including a grand feast at which cattle were sacrificed and their blood sprinkled over the food. Meanwhile, the participants filled their flagons with ale and made rousing toasts to the Nordic gods such as Odin or Freyr. Feasts like this took place three times a year – in the start of winter, when sacrifices were made to ensure sufficient food through the coming months; in midwinter, as a prelude to a successful harvest for the crops planted the following spring and in the spring, the season for Viking raiding expeditions when sacrifices were made to secure victory and an abundance of plunder.

Viking religious practices spread to Iceland, which was first colonized by Norwegians in AD874. A regular feature of Icelandic worship and one that continued long after Christianity was introduced, was the sacrifice made to the *landvaettir*, the land spirits. They were worshipped on hills, in woods and groves, or at waterfalls and stones. These were more personal, individual sacrifices, designed to enlist the landvaettir for good harvests and hunting or fishing expeditions.

Public sacrifices also took place in Iceland, notably at the annual assembly of the Icelandic Parliament, the Althing, at which a bull was sacrificed and its blood spread over the sacred ring used for swearing oaths. In around AD1000, Christian missionaries, sent from Norway by King Olaf I Trygvasson, arrived in Iceland and began the work of conversion. The Althing soon adopted Christianity, but this conversion came with a compromise: some pagan practices, including sacrifice, were allowed to continue. Icelanders were permitted to go on eating horsemeat, which was generally forbidden to Christians. Horses and pigs, the main sacrificial animals. were still slaughtered and cooked in a pit and their blood was spread over the idols and the walls at the temples.

However, though the sacrifices to the ancient gods continued, the Althing decreed that these had to be performed in secret. This was part of a halfway-house strategy, which also occurred elsewhere in Europe, in which Christianity was eased in to a pagan society rather than being imposed by force, giving us many of our present day festivals which, on closer examination, are a curious hybrid of the two. This served to smooth the way for the very difficult process of shedding age-old ideas deeply woven into the fabric of everyday life. One example of the 'semi-convert' was Raedwald, King of East Anglia between around AD599 and AD635, whose ancestry was Nordic. In his *Ecclesiastical History of the English People*, the Venerable Bede wrote of Raedwald that he '. . . tried to serve both Christ and the ancient gods, and he had in the same shrine an altar for the holy Sacrifice of Christ side by side with a small altar on which victims were offered to devils.'[11]

In Iceland, at least, Christianity was not entirely trusted to produce protection or success. One of the first settlers on the north Atlantic island, Helgi Eyvindarsson, used to pray to Christ in the safety of his home, but when out at sea, where all manner of dangers lurked, he preferred to invoke the powers of the ancient Norse god, Aegir. All the same, to be on the safe side, Helgi named his home in Iceland in honour of Christ: Kristnes, or Christ's headland.

This sort of compromise did not, of course, appeal to more militant Christians. Christianity came to Norway at around the same time as Iceland, as the Norwegian king, Olaf I Tryggvason embarked on a campaign of force and confrontation. Olaf was far less successful in Norway than his missionaries had been in Iceland. His efforts met considerable resistance and he sought to break this down by making terrible threats. Humans chosen for sacrifice in Scandinavia had

Detail from the Gundestrup Cauldron, Denmark. Knowledge of Celtic rituals is based on Roman accounts and heavily biased. Heads were collected in battle and human sacrifices performed by the priestly caste of Druids in wooded groves dedicated to a variety of gods, including the warrior goddess, Andraste. (See: *The Gods of the Celts*, Sutton, 2000)

Werner Forman

generally come from the dross of society – thieves, murderers and other criminals and slaves. King Olaf proposed instead to sacrifice high-ranking men and leaders. Even this did not overcome all opposition, and Christianizing success was largely confined to the coastal areas of Norway. The work was completed, however, by another Olaf, King Olaf II Haraldsson, the future St Olaf, who created the church of Norway in 1024.

Sweden was a much tougher proposition. A third Olaf, King Olaf Skštkonung, who became King of Sweden in AD990, was a devout and militant Christian, but he was successfully defied by the pagan chiefs, who managed to fend off Christianization for two centuries. The focus of pagan worship in Sweden was Uppsala, where every nine years, human and animal sacrifices were made. Sometime in the eleventh century, Adam of Bremen, a German geographer and writer, described what happened:

'The sacrifice is as follows: of every living creature they offer nine head, and with the blood of those, it is the custom to placate the gods, but the bodies are hanging in a grove which is near the temple; so holy is that grove to the heathens that each tree in it is presumed to be divine by reason of the victim's death and putrefaction. There are also dogs and horses hung along with men. . . . The sacrifice was made at the beginning of summer, the traditional time of offerings to Odin, in return for victory in the coming season.'[12]

These and similar pagan practices continued in Sweden long after the lifetime of Adam of Bremen. Christianity was not established there until around 1164, when the first archbishop was consecrated. The task had been completed by the persuasions of missionaries from elsewhere in Europe, but instant Christianization by force had still been a frequent feature of the process. It often led to open – and ferocious war – as Christians and pagans fought for supremacy. Pagan temples, their altars and their idols were destroyed and Christian churches were burned in response. In AD782, the Frankish Emperor Charlemagne had 4,500 Saxon prisoners slaughtered for refusing to become Christians. Charlemagne afterwards decreed the death penalty for those who refused to be baptised or persisted with the pagan faith. Church councils repeatedly called for an end to pagan practices in Germany, together with the wearing of amulets and in particular the offering of sacrifices to the new Christian saints who had taken the place of the ancient pagan gods. It was a full-scale ideological war, though longstanding political rivalries, for instance between the Saxons and the Franks, were being aired at the same time.[13]

Nevertheless, the further reaches of Europe – towards the east – remained untouched for quite some time. Perun, the Slavic storm god, was worshipped in sacred oak groves of present day Poland, the Czech Republic and Slovakia, and in Russia, where Orthodox Christianity was not introduced until AD988, sacrifices were offered to him or his Christian equivalent, St Ilya, every 20 July until well into the nineteenth century. Sacrifices to Perun consisted of cockerels, goats, bulls and bears, and the oak tree was considered sacred to him.

In central Russia, in the region around the Ural Mountains, the sacred grove – this time a grove of deciduous trees – figured once again as the site of the *mer*, an important pagan festival, with sacrifices held every five years or so among the Votyaks. The significance of the grove was that the village ancestors had once worshipped there. The meaning of mer was 'village community' and when the time arrived, several villages would attend to perform animal sacrifices to the gods of nature. White animals were sacrificed to the nature gods, and the accompanying prayers were made in a southerly direction. Conifer trees, too, had a supernatural aura, and it was in their vicinity, with prayers made towards the north, that black animals were sacrificed to the dead and the guardian spirits of the earth. These guardians watched over individual households as well as certain areas of land. Rituals and sacrifices for the dead were an occasion for venerating the ancestors who safeguarded family welfare and ensured the wellbeing and continuing prosperity of the family group.

Further south, around Kiev, where Swedish Vikings had settled in the area named Rus, a more recognizably Nordic ceremony – a ship burial – was observed in AD921, by the Muslim Arab traveller, Ahmed Ibn Fadlan:

'The burial featured the corpse of a chieftain dressed in sumptuous silk and brocade and surrounded by grave-offerings of food, drink and herbs. A dog, two chickens, cows and two horses were then sacrificed and thrown in pieces on to the ship. Another, human sacrifice – a slave girl – was strangled and stabbed and also placed on the vessel. The ship was then set on fire.'[14]

The horses sacrificed at Rus were probably intended as the dead chieftain's guards. This type of sacrifice was connected with worship of the Norse god Odin, chief of the gods and god of battle, and the flesh was a frequent feature of sacred meals in northern Europe. It was still customary in pagan Denmark for two centuries after Ibn Fadlan went to Rus, and also spread to some areas conquered or settled by the Vikings during their shock expansion out of Scandinavia after the eighth century AD. When the Plantagenet King John of England was buried in 1216, horses were slaughtered for the occasion, and the same rite was observed at the obsequies of the Holy Roman Emperor Charles IV in 1378 and of Bertrand Du Guesclin, French hero of the Hundred Years' War, in 1380.

The sacrifice of horses was used, too, to provide guardians for newly-erected buildings, and in 1318, well into Christian times in Europe, a horse was killed for the foundation of the monastery at Kšnigsfelden in Germany. This particular pagan custom long outlived the establishment of Christian supremacy in Europe and appears to have been a defence against witchcraft and evil. As recently as 1897, a horse's head was buried in the foundations of a Methodist chapel in the fens of Cambridgeshire, and a libation of beer poured over it before it was sealed in behind the bricks and mortar of the building.[15]

The sacrifice of horses and the ritual consumption of their flesh naturally met ferocious opposition from Christians, but even the strongly worded edict issued by Pope Gregory III in the mid-eighth century AD, condemning the eating of horseflesh as 'an unclean and execrable act' failed to put a stop to the practice. Even where Christianity seemed to establish itself, the devotion of the newly converted could be shallow and no more than a front for secret pagan worship. In 1251, Grand Duke Mindaugas of Lithuania ostensibly became a Christian, but according to the *Galician-Livonian Chronicle*, behind the scenes and sometimes openly,

'. . . he made sacrifices to the gods – Nenadey, Telyavel, Diveriks, the hare-god and (the goddess of the forest) Meiden. When Mindaugas rode out into the field and a hare ran across his path . . . he made sacrifices to his god, burned corpses and conducted pagan rites in public'.[16]

Mindaugas was a surprising candidate for conversion, for he had unified his duchy for the specific purpose of halting the spread of Christianity and resisting the Christian armies that aimed to enforce it. Although there was a certain amount of Christian infiltration and the sort of dual worship Mindaugas himself practised, Lithuania was to all intents and purposes a strongly cohesive state with a governing bureaucracy in full control, and a national religion that was able to challenge the Christian infrastructure as introduced in other lands. The pagan pantheon of Lithuania came complete with pagan symbolism, festivals and sacrificial practices. There were two harvest festivals where a goat was sacrificed. Sacrifices of pigs were made to the water god Upinis and black suckling pigs to the earth goddess Zemyna. Afterwards, the meat of the sacrifice was used to make sandwiches with the first bread of the harvest and presented to Zemyna in private.

Lithuania, which eventually stretched from the Baltic to the Black Sea, was the stronghold of organized paganism in Europe, and flourished as reassurance to hard-pressed pagans elsewhere that the ancient ways had not yet submitted to the new Christian imperative. Ironically, political pressures succeeded in Christianizing Lithuania, where missionaries and armies had failed. In 1384, a marriage was arranged between the Lithuanian Grand Duke Jogaila and the ten-year old Queen Jadwiga of Poland. Poland was then contesting territory with Hungary and needed a strong adult ruler rather than a child to lead the struggle.

The Polish plan dovetailed with Jogaila's own expansionist aims and he was duly elected King of Poland on 2 February 1386. One condition of the marriage, which took place the following 18 February, was that he should convert to Christianity. Three days before the wedding, Jogaila was baptized as Wladyslaw III. Afterwards, he commanded that his subjects follow his lead and Lithuania became the last pagan state in Europe to turn officially Christian.

7

Heart of the Matter: Central and South America

With the conversion of Lithuania, the first phase of Christianization came to an end. The next did not begin for another century and a half, when the scene of operations shifted to an environment that could not have been more different from that of Europe: the Americas. The Spaniards who followed in the wake of Christopher Columbus from the early sixteenth century onwards discovered that America was a New World in more ways than one: much more vast, even more varied, with a long spine of mountains a quarter as high again as any in Europe and, in addition, a number of active volcanoes.

The presence of these volcanoes, sited mainly along the western coast of North and South America and in and around the Valley of Mexico, made the gods of pagan America seem particularly ferocious and vengeful. Consequently, religious sacrifices, especially in central America, expressed human terror at the furious mood of the gods in extreme and lurid terms and produced frantic efforts at pacifying the mighty powers that made for such a volatile environment. It was not in the least surprising that the Aztecs, who conquered a vast empire in Mexico before the Spaniards arrived, conceived the creation of the world as a series of destructions, requiring the Earth, all its living creatures, all its flora and the Sun to be recreated several times.

The native Americans in the north, in the present day United States and Canada, were much more favoured by Nature. Her copious bounty enabled them to perpetuate a hunting culture long after it had died out elsewhere. On the Plains of the southwest, the buffalo supplied them

79

Tom Bean

A Pueblo (meso-American) people, the Anasazi founded a civilization in southern Utah, AD0–1300. They built multi-storey complexes of brick and laid straight, paved roads. Their wealth came from trading in precious stones and pottery, such as those 'sacrificed' in this ritual burial. Latest evidence suggests they may also have practised cannibalism.

with virtually everything they needed to live – food, hides for clothing, tipis, and bones for their tools. As a result, North America never gave rise to ancient urban civilizations like those of the Incas in Peru or Aztecs in Mexico, where resources had to be carefully husbanded and the state and its needs had to be served by obedient populations.

Instead, the native North Americans were generally tribal and semi-nomadic and their religion was largely shamanistic. The shaman was called in to ensure a successful hunt, a good harvest or a victory over enemies. Religious rituals, including sacrifice, also had a place as the natives of North America sought to propitiate angry gods. However, they lived too close to Nature and had such a symbiotic relationship with animals that their form of sacrifice did not involve the violence and bloodshed practised elsewhere.

80

Individuals would offer furs, tobacco or food to placate the gods. They had a very strong affinity with the animals they hunted, most especially the buffalo who, they believed, shared a common ancestry with them. In these circumstances, religious sacrifice was generally more symbolic than actual. For instance, in the important Sun Dance performed by various Plains tribes, sacrifice took the form of self-inflicted thirst, hunger and pain. Among the Sioux and Cheyenne of the Plains, the dancers' flesh was torn by skewers or they were suspended from the roof of the ceremonial lodge by thongs attached to skewers which passed through their chests or backs. This was not masochism, but an effort by the dancers to return some part of themselves to Nature in exchange for benefits, both past and future.

These and other religious practices remained largely untouched by Europeans until the seventeenth century. However, European presence intruded into central and South America at a much earlier date. The Spaniards were quite different from the generally tolerant English, French, Dutch and Portuguese, who came to the present day United States and Canada for purposes of trade or religious freedom. The Spanish, too, came for gold and riches, but an equally powerful mission was to convert the heathen to Christianity.

When the conquistadors, led by Hernan Cortes, made the first appreciable penetration of the New World in 1519, Spain was the focus of Christianity at its most devout and self-confident. Its fires of faith were fuelled by a long, but successful struggle against the Muslim Moors who had occupied Iberia for nearly eight centuries. Christianity was therefore at a peak of militant zeal when, in Aztec Mexico, it encountered native American paganism at its most bloodstained and frenetic.

Fear and dread was implicit in Aztec religious belief, for to them, another destruction of the world was always imminent. Aztecs believed that they lived in the era of the Fifth Sun, the fifth creation of the world, which would one day be destroyed by sky monsters. The end of every 52-year cycle was a most dangerous time, a time when the world was most likely to come to an end and the fate of Earth was written in the behaviour of a single star, Aldebaran in the constellation Taurus. If

A funerary anthropomorphic figurine from Teotihuacan, Mexico. The hole in the midriff shows where the 'heart' was removed and may have been for touching, to bestow luck.

Gianni Dalli Orti

the star failed to move on the night it reached its zenith, then destruction would follow. If it moved, the world would survive for another 52 years, when the whole fearful process would begin again. Before that night of suspense and trepidation, as Aldebaran approached its zenith, the Aztecs offered their goods to the gods or the sacrifice of blood, drawn from their ears and tongues. After the crisis was over and Aldebaran continued on its path across the heavens, the Aztec priests would light the first fires that had burned in Mexico for twelve days, and offer a human sacrifice as thanksgiving.[1]

For Aztec priests, sacrificing their own blood was a daily occurrence. They used cactus spines to make their ears, tongues, thighs and genitals bleed as offerings to the gods. The most important of these gods was Huitzilopochtli, the Sun, on whom the Aztec world depended for much more than the traditional 52-year cycle. He was responsible for nothing less than daily existence for, if he did not have the strength to rise each morning, then the world would be destroyed. The way to prevent that, in Aztec thinking, was to make human sacrifices to the Sun on a daily basis.

The Aztec concept of human sacrifice and its purpose originated three centuries before the arrival of the Spaniards, at a time when they were a poor, semi-nomadic tribe of pariahs, spurned by other Mexicans for their ferocity and for ever moving on in search of a land of their own. During their wanderings, as the *Tira de la Peregrinacion*[2] relates, the Aztecs came across three bodies lying on cacti: the chests of all three had been torn open and their hearts removed. This set the pattern for Aztec human sacrifice after they reached the home Huitzilopochtli had promised them, in 1325 or 1345, on the shore of Lake Texcoco in the Valley of Mexico.[3] By the time the Spaniards reached the Valley, human sacrifice was a well-established practice in the magnificent city of Tenochtitlan, the 'place of the prickly pear cactus' which the Aztecs had built in the middle of the Lake.

To the Spaniards, of course, human sacrifice – as opposed to simple murder – was utterly repugnant. The Aztec viewpoint was quite different: the Sun had to be nourished with human hearts and this view was shared even among the sacrifices themselves. To be sacrificed to the Sun was, to them, a great honour, a means of achieving divinity and something else that might never have otherwise come their way – translation after death to the Paradise of the Sun normally reserved for great warriors or women who had died in childbirth. On occasion, the Spaniards were able to save victims from death on the sacrificial altar, only to be utterly confounded when these same victims proved ungrateful and demanded to be sacrificed.

Each sacrifice died on the altar for the sake of a particular god. Their name, *ixiptla*, meant 'god's image' and after ceremonial bathing, they were dressed in the robes and badges of their deity. The sacrifices took place at the top of a tower 2.5 metres high, requiring the ixiptla to climb a steep staircase to reach the summit. Once there, he was seized, and spread out on the altar with four priests holding his arms and legs and another his head. Death came swiftly. The *tlenamacac*, the élite priest whose task it was to make the sacrifice, cut the chest open in one swift movement with an obsidian-bladed knife, tore out the heart, still beating, and held it up as an offering to the Sun. Afterwards, the body was rolled down the steps, staining them red as it went. Later, the flesh was eaten and the skull was placed in a *zompantl*, or skull rack.

Bernal Diaz del Castillo, one of the conquistadors who went to Mexico with Hernan Cortes, and the last survivor of the expedition, wrote his memoirs when he was over seventy years of age, in around 1562. Time, it was evident, had not dimmed the impact the aftermath of Aztec human sacrifice made on him:

'They cut off the arms, thighs, and head, eating the arms and thighs at their ceremonial banquets. The head they hang up on a beam and the body of the sacrificed man is not eaten, but given to beasts of prey . . . (Snakes) were fed on the bodies of (the) sacrificed and the flesh of the dogs that they had bred. . . . These snakes were dedicated to their fierce idols and kept them company. . . . It was so appalling that one seemed to be in Hell.'4

Just as hellish to the Spaniards was the appearance of the tlenamacac priests who performed human sacrifice and painted their faces black. According to Hernan Cortes, they never washed their hair or clothes, but left them thickly matted with the blood they spilled in such profusion.5 In the first of the four reports Hernan Cortes wrote to King Charles I in Spain, he estimated the numbers of human sacrifices that were made in Aztec Mexico:

'This land seems to us to be very large and to have many temples in it. Not one year has passed, as far as we have been able to discover, in which three or four thousand souls have not been sacrificed.'6

By Cortes' reckoning, between ten and fifty thousand people a year were sacrificed to the Sun in Mexico. However, thousands more could be slaughtered at one time on special occasions, such as the dedication in 1487 of the twin temples of Huitzolopochtli and Quetzalcoatl, the 'bringer of civilisation', when 20,000 humans were sacrificed over a period of four days. Many of them came to Tenochtitlan as part of the tribute due

Gianni Dalli Orti

Aztec stoneware container for hearts, in the shape of an eagle. The bird would carry the soul of the departed sacrifice up to the sun god, Huitzilopochtli.

from the provinces of the Aztec empire, some were prisoners of war, others were slaves. They stood in four lines, stretching over 3 km through the streets of Tenochtitlan, waiting their turn as enthusiastic crowds milled about watching the spectacle that would ensure their daily survival.

However, Huitzilopochtli was only the greatest and most demanding of the Aztec gods. Xipe Totec, the Flayed Lord, a god of rain and springtime, received sacrifices when prisoners were shot to death with arrows: afterwards, their blood dripped on the ground, so nourishing it. Other sacrifices to Xipe Totec had to fight four opponents while tied to a large stone and equipped with dummy weapons, one of which was a sword edged with down instead of the usual sharp obsidian. If his four attackers, who were armed with real weapons, did not manage to kill

85

him, the sacrifice was dispatched by a fifth, who was left-handed. The flayed skin of the dead man was worn by his killer, in imitation of Xipe Totec, for twenty days. At the festival of Xilonen, the goddess of growing corn, a slave girl was decapitated, a form of sacrifice reserved for women impersonating goddesses: this represented harvested maize heads. The ceremony in honour of the Xiuhtechtli, the fire god, involved throwing prisoners on to a fire, dragging them off with hooks while still alive and then removing their hearts.

The Aztec rain-god, Tlaloc, was induced to send rain through the deaths of very young children who were drowned or taken to mountain peaks and walled up in caves. The copious weeping of these terrified children was considered a good sign for success: the more the children cried, the more the Aztecs believed it would rain. These sacrifices were regular occurrences, performed in the first and third months of the Aztec year, which lasted for eighteen months in all. Each month had its own festival, but few were more spectacular than the Festival of Tezcatlipoca, the creator-god.

For this festival, which took place in the fifth month, a young man of sixteen or seventeen was chosen to impersonate Tezcatlipoca. The choice was made a year in advance and this last year of the young man's life was a time of pampering and luxury. He was taught how to play the flute, wore splendid garments, gold bangles to decorate his arms and gold bells to wear around his legs. He was garlanded with flowers and had eight attendants to wait on him and grant his every wish. Twenty days before the festival, the young man was dressed as a warrior chieftain, and a fortnight later, everyone took part in five days of feasting, dancing and celebration. On the day of the festival itself, the young 'Tezcatlipoca' stepped in to a canoe and was paddled to a small temple on the shore of Lake Texcoco. From there he walked towards the temple and as he climbed the steps, he broke each of the flutes he had played during his year of leisure and pleasure. Then, on reaching the top, he was sacrificed.

As soon as his heart had been ripped out, another boy of the same age, destined to die at the next festival, was chosen to take his place.

The Aztecs did not initiate human sacrifice in Mexico. It was performed several centuries before they came to power, at El Tajin, at

Mictecacihuatl was the Aztec Goddess of Death, although this figurine seems more likely to have been a doll to scare naughty children.

Gianni Dalli Orti

Veracruz on the east coast between about AD600 and AD900. Human sacrifice later appeared among the Toltecs, Zapotecs, Tarascans, Mayas and other tribes and the Mayas were, if anything, even more ferocious in the practice than the Aztecs. Their art depicted scenes of preliminary mutilation, disembowelling, scalping, slow bleeding and other tortures before the actual sacrifice was made. Some sacrifices had their nails torn out, as illustrated in the murals excavated at Bonampak in the present day Mexican state of Chiapas, where figures were shown with blood spurting from the ends of their fingers.[7]

In the Yucatan peninsula on the south east coast of Mexico, the Ah Kin, whose name meant 'he of the Sun' presided over human sacrifices. The actual performance of sacrifice was the task of the Nacom, who was aided by four old men known as Chacs. They held down the victim's limbs as the Nacom opened the chest and retrieved the heart. The sacrifices were usually prisoners, slaves or illegitimate children and

87

Detail from the *bas* relief in the Ball Court at Chichen Itza, Yucatan. The game, played mostly with a rubber ball, may have had religious significance. The captain of the winning team is depicted holding a severed head, thought to be an effigy of the High Priest of Cuzco, the Inca capital. The carving behind him is the plumed serpent, Quetzalcoatl.

orphans who were purchased specifically for the purpose. Animals, birds and insects were also sacrificed, and there was in addition, a bloodless practice in which flowers, rubber or jade were offered. Even so, the fury of blood sacrifice was never far away, for like the Aztecs, the Mayas practised self-mutilation during rituals, using needles or the spines of the stingray to pierce their ears, lips, tongues, cheeks or genitals to draw blood. The blood was afterwards spread over the idols of the gods.

To preserve water, the most precious commodity in the Yucatan, sacrificial victims were thrown into a *cenote*, a deep natural well at Chichen Itza. The purpose was to produce rain to feed the cenote and, as additional inducements, copper, gold and jade were also sacrificed. If the human sacrifice managed to survive the experience, it was believed that he had communed with the gods and brought back a divine message concerning the fate of the year's crops.

By contrast to the Maya and the Aztecs, the Inca civilization in Peru, which straddled the high Andes of western South America, was relatively mild in its religious observances. This may have arisen from the fact that Tahuantinsuyu, the Land of the Four Quarters, was a far more subdued society than Aztec Mexico, with a Sapa Inca who was regarded as the Son of the Sun, owner of everyone and everything under the sun. Obedience to the Sapa Inca was automatic and unthinking. All Incas were born to their roles in life, which could never be changed, with traditional duties that had to be observed and daily tasks that had to be performed. Basic needs were provided by the state. Although sacrifice took place in Peru, including human sacrifice, it lacked the desperate zeal of the Aztec practice and the sadism of the Mayan.

The deeply conservative and conformist ethos of Inca Peru extended even to the making of sacrifices, which were paid for by compulsory public taxes. Each of the Inca gods had their own type of offerings and rituals, though in every case Viracocha, the creator god, was addressed first. All forms of sacrifice were strictly preordained. Father Bernabe Cobo, one of the many Spaniards who wrote of their experiences in America, observed that:

'The form to be followed in the sacrifices was so well established, with the rites and ceremonies designated for each one, that no one was permitted to exercise his own free will in changing, adding or eliminating anything from what was ordained. . . . At every town and *huaca* (sacred place), attendants were assigned for each sacrifice, and it was stipulated when each sacrifice was to be made, the form and manner in which it was to be carried out. . .'[8]

From the critical, Spanish Catholic point of view, the Incas were so greatly in thrall to their gods that they were willing to sacrifice to them all or anything they possessed. This, according to Bernabe Cobo, included 'everything from the children they begat to the fruits of their harvests'. Inca sacrifices certainly covered a wide range of offerings –

Macduff Everton

A 'stairway to the stars', literally, for the human sacrifices of the Maya. The double-pyramid of Tikal, the largest known Maya city, lies in what is now Guatemala. Tikal was suddenly abandoned in about AD800, possibly because of severe drought, and never reoccupied. Visitors to the ruins speak of a brooding atmosphere even to this day.

The Moche of northern Peru vanished about AD800. They left thousands of pottery objects of the highest quality, together with raised burials and buildings demonstrating architectural knowledge. They also practised human sacrifice. This painted and glazed cup however depicts a priest about to offer a chicken.

coca leaves, maize, gold and silver ornaments, carved and scented woods, eyebrow hair, eyelashes, food, vegetable flour, red ochre, seashells and various plants. As in other pagan societies, however, the most important offering was blood, although, as Cobe admitted, the ultimate offering – human sacrifice – was not a frequent occurrence in Peru, since the occasions that demanded it were relatively rare.

Like the Aztecs in Mexico, human sacrifice in Peru did not originate with the Incas. It was a well established form of sacrifice six hundred years and more before the Incas conquered their vast empire. Among the Mochica, whose civilization dominated the northern coast of Peru between the first and the eighth centuries AD, prisoners of war were sacrificed and their blood was ritually drunk. In 1995, stark evidence of this and other similar Mochica practices was uncovered by archaeologists at the Huaca de la Luna, the Temple of the Moon, at the city of Moche, where 42 skeletons of sacrificed young men were found. Many had large fractures to their skulls and had evidently been bludgeoned to death.

Leonard di Selva

French print from the nineteenth century depicting an 'Inca sacrifice'. The figure on the left entreating the woman to offer up her child, and the piece of unidentifiable offal being handed to the acolyte on the right, lend realism to this otherwise heavily idealized composition.

This, though, was not part of regular mass sacrifice. The thick sedimentary layers in which the skeletons were found indicated that the offerings were confined to the season of heavy rains and had been made over a number of years. The purpose, it appears, was to secure fertility of the crops and the preservation of Mochica society.

Much later, in Inca Peru, human sacrifice was also limited. It was considered necessary at times of famine, war, earthquakes or pestilence. The most frequent sacrifices were children, mainly girls aged around ten years old and also spotless virgins aged up to sixteen. To qualify as a sacrifice, they had to be physically perfect, without a blemish or even a mole on their bodies. Parents, mindful of the public good, would offer these children for sacrifice of their own free will. Some, however, seem to have arranged for their daughters to escape this fate: they saw to it that they were disqualified by being seduced at an early age.

Before death, the children were well treated and given plenty to eat and drink, so that when they reached the next world they would not be hungry or unhappy. Infants, who were also included among the sacrifices, were breast-fed by their mothers. When the time came, they were taken two or three times around the idols of the gods and then, wrote Bernabe Cobo:

'They were sacrificed by being strangled with a cord or by having their throats slit. Some had their hearts cut out, and while they were still beating, their hearts were offered to the gods to whom the sacrifice was directed. The faces of the idols and the embalmed bodies of the lords and kings were smeared with the blood of those whose hearts were cut out, and that of those whose throats were cut. This was done when the offering was made and a line was made on the face of the idol or embalmed body from ear to ear across the middle of the nose.'[9]

Many of these child sacrifices took place high in the Andes, at or near the peaks of the snow-capped mountains. This lonely environment was ideal for the preservation of their remains. Towards the end of the last century, several discoveries of complete sacrifices were made by archaeologists working at nearly 7 km altitude on soaring mountain crags in the thin and freezing air. In September 1995, a hiker came across the frozen body of a girl aged about eight on the Nevado Ampato volcano. She had been sacrificed at least five hundred years previously. Later X-ray examination revealed that she had died from a mighty blow to the head which cracked her skull just above her right eye and caused severe bleeding to the brain.

Two years later, it was announced that six frozen mummies had been found near the crater of the 5,821 m high El Misti volcano, some 750 km southeast of Lima. The bodies lay in two graves, together with ceremonial pots, gold and silver statuettes and cloth blankets which showed signs of having been burned by volcanic eruptions. The find was no surprise: El Misti already had a reputation as the world's most prolific mountain site

Dave Bartruff

A Nazca open-air ritual burial, on the high plains of Peru.

for human sacrifices among the many Andean sites where children were killed for the sake of the gods and the prosperity of Tahuantinsuyu.

Since 1983, the American-Argentine-Peruvian expedition sponsored by the National Geographical Society had been excavating in the Andes and had already uncovered sixteen mummified bodies of Inca sacrifices before the discovery in 1999 of three small children at the peak of the Llullaillaco volcano. The two girls and one boy were aged between eight and fifteen years. One of them wore a headdress decorated with white feathers and a geometrically-patterned yellow cloak. The bodies were so remarkably preserved that the fingernails and fine hairs on the arms were still in perfect condition.

94

The Inca 'sacrificial altar' at Machu Picchu, Peru. This unique UNESCO 'World Heritage' site (see also back cover) is itself about to be sacrificed to commercial development, with plans to construct a large tourist hotel complex and chair lift.

Wolfgang Kaehler

These and all other sacrifices in Tahuantinsuyu, were accompanied by prayers for the wellbeing of the Sapa Inca who was himself the subject of special offerings. At his coronation, up to 200 children would be sacrificed. More sacrifices were made when the Sapa Inca went to war or became ill. It was also a custom in Peru for a father who feared he was dying to offer his own son as a sacrifice to Viracocha or to Inti, the sun-god, in order to escape death himself. A further occasion of sacrifice was the Sun Festival, Inti Raymi, which lasted for a month. Once again, the sacrifices were children, this time between 10 and 12 years old, who were ceremonially led round a huge idol depicting Inti and were then buried alive with silver objects, llamas and ground sea shells. The sacrifice was followed by a grand banquet in Cuzco's main square.

95

Animal sacrifices in Peru were confined to domesticated animals, which in effect meant llamas and to a lesser extent, alpacas and guinea pigs. Wild animals were not generally considered suitable for sacrifice, for it was felt that these creatures, reared by Nature, as it were, had not required the same personal care from those who were offering them to the gods. This was not an absolute rule, however, for the Incas sacrificed birds and, as Bernabe Cobo put it, 'a thousand other things that grew up in the wild without any human assistance.'

Offerings usually became eligible for sacrifice to particular gods because of their colour or markings. Brown-coated llamas were offered to Viracocha and white llamas to Inti. Smooth-furred llamas and woolly alpacas were sacrificed to Inti as a special plea for the fertility of the land. This last ceremony was performed on a daily basis in Cuzco, the Inca capital. Before the sacrifice, the presiding priest turned the animal's head so that it was looking directly at the idol and then cut its throat. Finally, dressed in a red vest, the llama was burned in what was called the Sun's offering. As it burned, baskets of coca-leaves were thrown into the fire.

In addition, the Sun was fed at a sacrifice that took place every morning: a fire of carved wood was lit and some of the prepared food was thrown in and burned. The rest was eaten by the priests and their attendants. In similar vein, part-coloured llamas were sacrificed to Apu Illapu, the rain god, to induce him to release rain from the Milky Way constellation, where Incas believed it was stored.

Sacrifice in Tahuantinsuyu also had its part to play in augury. The bodies of sacrificed guinea pigs were sliced open and the innards studied, a ritual also performed on some sacrifice llamas. Particularly elaborate sacrifices accompanied preparations for war, when they were used to 'weaken' the enemy and so ensure victory. Bernabe Cobo described one form of this sacrifice:

'Then, the (Incas) brought out some black (llamas) that had been kept in prison with nothing to eat for several days, and they killed them, saying that in the same way that the hearts of those animals were weakened, so may their enemies lose heart.'10

96

Another Mochica 'toby jug' depicts the sky god, Aia-Paec. As with the previous image of the priest, curious, tusk-like teeth are prominent, possibly evidence of a boar cult; the god is wearing a nose ring rather than a lip disc and the feathered war bonnet is reminiscent of later American plains Indians.

Charles & Josette Lenars

These and all other pagan practices in the Americas came to an end with the Spanish conquest, though this conquest was very protracted. Mexico was subjugated after 1521 and Peru after 1532. The Mayas in southeast Mexico and Guatemala managed to hold out in the unreachable depths of their forests and jungles until 1697.[11] This loss of freedom was accompanied by the most fundamental loss of all: the Spaniards destroyed the native religions, smashed their idols, tore down the temples and banned the sacrifices, especially human sacrifices, and all the pagan rituals and festivals. In their place, they imposed Christianity and built churches on the sites of ruined temples. The most complete single

Gianni Dalli Orti

The Tzompantli altar at Chichen Itza depicts hundreds of ornately carved skulls. Not without grim humour, each skull represents the soul of a departed Maya sacrifice.

destruction occurred at the start, at Tenochtitlan, where the city was laid waste in the siege that finally saw the end of the Aztec rule in 1521.

However, what the Spaniards could not destroy or effectively prohibit was ancient belief, and human sacrifice continued in Mexico for some time, though in secret. Human sacrifice also persisted among the Maya, but with curious acknowledgement to the new religion. As late as 1868, these sacrifices were still being performed, either in the traditional Mayan fashion, with removal of the heart, or by crucifixion. And in Peru, the festival of the Sun, Inti Raymi, is still held at Cuzco and the nearby Inca fortress of Sacsuahaman on 24 June every year. Until 1997, a white llama was sacrificed in the traditional way but humanitarian protests have since seen to it that the 'heart' afterwards held up by the Inca 'high priest' was a fake.

8

A Darker Continent: Africa

Africa is not homogeneous. A continent of enormous variety, it contains hundreds of different tribes, and as many different customs, languages, beliefs and religious practices. Though reports by Christian missionaries and other travellers in Africa in the nineteenth century were exaggerated, their picture of a populace living in fear of malevolent forces was not entirely inaccurate. In these circumstances, the witchcraft, sorcery, magic, and shamanistic practices that sought to control the situation were natural choices for people who lived so close to Nature and her depredations. Prayer was an ongoing practice, at any time, in any place, even before entering a shrine for more formal worship. Altars were set up in homes as well as public places. Sacred places were sited in caves, on mountains, at crossroads, on thresholds, river banks, waterfalls, rocks and around trees. Spirits inhabited woods and forests, mountains, rivers and areas around villages. In fact, from the African viewpoint, the entire universe was one vast spiritual area, religious in all its many aspects.

Sacrifice was naturally prominent in this scenario and the perfection that was God required very strict rules in performing it. Animals chosen for sacrifice had to be of one colour only. Black or white was considered desirable. Priests conducting sacrifices needed to be untainted by the grosser human concerns: sex, food and other worldly activities.[1] Various African tribes offered sacrifices in every conceivable circumstance — when there was too little rain, when there was too much, at weddings, at the start of pregnancy, birth, naming, circumcision, funerals, planting time, ripening time, harvest time, to cleanse a village or area after an epidemic, while gathering fruit, after a successful hunt, to ward off or appease evil spirits or simply to express gratitude to God for a good harvest or recovery from an accident. The materials offered were just as varied: eggs, wine, portions of meat, honey, fruits, water, poppy or sesame seeds, maize, millett, leaves, milk, beer, wine, money, incense, agricultural tools, tobacco, cowrie-shells even the dung of the hyrax, and the smoke of the first pipe of the morning.

Domestic animals, such as chickens, were sacrificed; though cattle, regarded as sacred by many tribes in Africa, were sacrificed and eaten only on religious occasions. Among the Dinka in southern Sudan, bulls and oxen were regarded as animals fated by God for sacrifice. Dogs were sacrificed every two weeks by blacksmiths of the Yoruba tribe in West Africa. Human sacrifice was performed in Africa, but only on rare occasions. One of these was severe drought, when the Akamba tribe of Kenya used to sacrifice a child by burying it alive at a shrine.

In Africa, God's function as an omnipotent power controlling the forces of Nature was incorporated into his name. The Kiga of Uganda, for instance, refer to God as 'The one who makes the sun set'. The Kikuyu of Kenya offered sacrifices for rain to the 'One who makes mountains quake and rivers overflow.' The Abaluya of Kenya call God 'One to whom sacred rites and sacrifices are made or paid'.[2]

This, though, did not exclude the worship of other powers. In eastern Africa, for example, there was widespread worship of ancestors as protectors of the people and sacrifices were made to them by the Bari tribe of Jubaland, in southern Sudan, or the Ankore of Uganda. The Ankore believed that God required no sacrifices: their offerings went instead to spirits and other deities as well as to their own ancestors. So were sacrifices offered by another Ugandan tribe, the Baganda.

Despite differences in detail, the pagan religions of Africa south of the Sahara Desert were based on animism, which ascribed souls to animals, inanimate objects and natural phenomena. However, the great geographical divide of the Sahara Desert made a considerable difference between religious beliefs and practice north and south of this largest desert in the world, nearly 8 million sq km in area. The north more properly belonged to the world of the Mediterranean and the Middle East. In Nubia in the northeast at around 1630BC, Ancient Egyptian practice was clearly the model when chieftains were buried in huge mounds surrounded by hundreds of retainers who had been sacrificed so that they could accompany him into the next world. Rather later, as the largest and best-known centre of pagan religion in this area, the city of Carthage followed the general lines already established by the religions of Mesopotamia and Greece.

Carthage was a trading city, founded around the Cape Bon Peninsula in 814BC on a site that is now a suburb of Tunis. It was one of several colonies established around the Mediterranean by the Phoenicians from Lebanon and Syria, who were, in their time, the most intrepid navigators, traders and explorers in the ancient world. Subsequently, the Carthaginians emulated this success, ultimately creating a rich trading empire that extended into Spain and possibly reached down the west coast of Africa. Worship in the Phoenician colonies centred around a family of gods. In Carthage, the family was headed by Baal-Hammon, the creator god also called El, and later by Tanit, the chief goddess. Unlike the animist faiths of the south, which attracted adherents through spiritual appeal, the religion of Carthage was a highly structured and formalized affair which operated on the principle that disaster was always pending and only the most frequent and, at times, most extreme sacrifices could avert calamity.

As in southern Africa, almost everything it was possible to sacrifice was offered to the gods: grain, flour, bread, fruits, wine, nuts of various kinds and poppy or sesame seeds and other foods all served as offerings. So did incense. It was the custom, too, for farmers and others to select sheep, goats, cows or oxen from their own flocks and bring them to the temple for sacrifice. On occasion, doves and pigeons were also offered.

A fourteenth century poem from northern Syria, detailing the sacrifice offered by the legendary King Keret, outlined the procedure:

'Enter the shade of a pavilion. Take a lamb in thy hand, A lamb of sacrifice in thy right hand; A kid in the grasp of both of them, All of thy food the choicest. Take a turtle dove, Bird of sacrifice. In a vessel of silver pour wine, Honey in a vessel of gold. Go up on the tower; And mount the shoulder of the wall; Lift up thy hands to heaven, Sacrifice to The Bull, thy father El; Honour Baal with thy sacrifice, The Son of Dagan with thine oblations'.

Human sacrifice in Phoenicia has been a controversial subject for some time. However, the most cogent evidence of this practice was not found there, but near Carthage, in a *tophet* or sanctuary at the small city of Kerkouane.

Sited on the tip of the Cap Bon peninsula, excavations at Kerkouane in 1985 and 1986, revealed thousands of urns containing the burned bones of infants. Pliny, Plutarch and other ancient writers came to the conclusion that human sacrifices were made to Baal at Carthage, and these remains would seem to bear them out.

It appears that poor parents in Carthage sold their children for sacrifice, though richer families were able to substitute slave children as their contribution. The sacrifices were performed to music, which drowned out the lamentations of the women present. The children were placed in the hands of a bronze idol and from there fell into a fire. As they burned, the heat transformed their faces into a fearful grimace, so giving the proceedings the name of 'ceremony of laughing'. The children in question were usually newly-born or stillborn or, later, they were aged up to three years old. From about the fifth century BC, sacrifices were of older children who were, presumably, better able to comprehend what was happening to them.

Whether or not human sacrifice took place in Carthage is a hotly debated issue, with some authorities claiming that the remains at Kerkouane indicate nothing more than a cemetery for children who died in the normal course of life. It has even been suggested that these sacrifices were a way of getting rid of unwanted children. This, however, leaves unexplained the votive *stelae* also found at the tophet which indicate intention to sacrifice: these stelae are typically inscribed 'To the Lady Tanit Pene Baal and the Lord Baal Hammon, that which (has been) vowed . . .' The fact of sacrifice has also been indicated by an image from one of the stelae showing a tall man in a long tunic, presumably a priestly tunic, carrying a naked infant. This has been interpreted as a picture of a priest carrying the sacrificial victim to the fire.

Another site, the tophet of the goddess Tanit on the hill of Byrsa which lay in the centre of Carthage, appears to have been specially constructed for the purpose of child sacrifice, probably the sacrifice of first-born children. At its greatest extent, the sanctuary covered more than 8,360 sq m. First probed in 1925, with further excavations in 1976–9, the site revealed urns full of the charred bones of children, goats, lambs and small birds. Some of the urns also contained jewellery – bracelets, rings, earrings, beads, amulets – and objects made of gold, silver, bronze and iron. In the tophet at Salammbo, excavated between 1974 and 1978, the urns were found to contain ashes and milk teeth from children who were probably sacrificed in the eighth century BC, not long after the foundation of Carthage.

It is also likely that mass sacrifice was performed at times of great danger for Carthage. In 310BC, during a war between Carthage and Syracuse in Sicily, Agathocles, tyrant of Syracuse in Sicily, landed an army on the coast and headed for the city. The Carthaginian response was to sacrifice 500 children from the best families by rolling them into the fire.[3] Another account has it that the children were strangled in the public square and were afterwards burned while the terrified citizens of Carthage looked on. Agathocles besieged Carthage for three years until the Carthaginians managed to break out and thrash his army. Subsequently, Agathocles fled back to Sicily.

Carthage eventually fell to Rome at the end of the Third Punic War in 146BC when the city was totally destroyed and its people were killed or sold into slavery. Subsequently, the city revived as a Roman foundation and a province of the Roman Empire. Finally, in around AD700, long after the fall of Rome, the area was conquered – and converted – by the forces of Islam. For all their energetic zeal, however, the Muslims did not find it nearly so easy to spread their faith through the rest of Africa. Islam filtered down the eastern and western coasts, usually in the wake of Arab traders. However, for a very long time, large areas of the impenetrable interior remained immune to conversion and even today, it is reckoned that around forty percent of Africans still practice some form of animism.

Mainstream Islam had little use for sacrifices and the subject rarely arose in the Qu'ran. Where it did, strict limitations were placed on the practice:

'And the beasts of sacrifice . . . we have appointed them for you as among God's waymarks; therein is good for you. So mention God's name over them, standing in ranks; then, when their flanks collapse, eat of them and feed the beggar and the suppliant. . . . The flesh of them shall not reach God, neither their blood, but godliness from you shall reach him. . .' .4

This, though, was not sufficient for tribes deeply imbued for centuries with beliefs in the ancient sacrifices. The Humr Baggarh and Fur peoples of the southern Sudan, both of them nominally Muslim, continued to use animistic offerings in order to ensure rainfall. To ensure fertility, the Fur used a form of libation, by pouring a paste of flour and water over their sanctuaries. Similar syncretism occurred among some Christian converts. Tribes like the Xhosas of South Africa accepted Christianity, but Africanized it. One Xhosa leader, the nineteenth century prophet, healer and diviner Nxele, was identified with Christ by his successor Mlandsheni, so reflecting the Messianic beliefs of both Jews and Christians, but not in the way intended by the missionaries who converted them.

On the other hand, the beliefs of the Sudanese Otoro and Azande had little or nothing to do with either Christian or Islamic monotheism. Their method of establishing justice and rooting out the guilty, for instance, was decidedly animist. They relied on charms, witchcraft, or rainmakers. The Azande in particular were experts at witchcraft, divination and oracles and vengeance magic, and considered that the ability to use all or any of these was inherited.

In matters of sacrifice, some very ancient ideas survived in Africa until quite recent times. The Bechuanas of Lesotho burned the stomach of an ox so that the black smoke rising would bring rain. Among the

Darrel Clowes

'Sacrificial altar' at the Temple of Amun, Merowe, Southern Sudan, c. 590BC. The Kushites established the 25th Dynasty of Pharaohs in Upper Egypt in about 700BC. They later retreated to Merowe as the Egyptian empire expanded and in AD543 converted to Christianity.

Boran people, who lived to the south of Ethiopia, children and cattle were sacrificed to the sky-spirit Wak. Wak was a truly fearsome deity. All children born within the first eight years or so of marriage belonged, not to their father, but to the sky-spirit and this meant that the infants had to be left in the bush to die. That done, their father was circumcised, which was regarded as a form of substitute-sacrifice releasing any future children from the ownership of Wak.[5] First-born males in Uganda suffered much the same fate in order to preserve the lives of their fathers, who would die if the children were not killed.

Human sacrifice for the sake of abundant crops was practised by the Marimo tribe of Bechuanaland. The offering was a short, stout man who was sometimes given strong drink to intoxicate him before he was carried off for sacrifice. He was killed in a wheat field where he was

105

Rock art has existed for 40,000 years, but its meaning is not always clear. Early cave paintings may represent votive offerings for a successful hunt. These rock paintings from Mali have a specific meaning: each records a circumcision ceremony, initiating a young Dogon male into adulthood.

believed to represent seed for the crops. Afterwards, his blood, his thorax, together with the attached flesh and his brain were burned. The resultant ashes were spread over the ground as fertilizer. The rest of the body served as a sacrificial meal.[6] Some sacrifices were conducted for brutally commercial reasons: the Kings of Dahomey in West Africa, for example, used to have a man drowned at the mouth of a river in order to bring merchants' ships into the area.

Another sacrifice for the sake of the harvest was performed in the area around present day Ruanda and Burundi, where a young girl who had reached the age of puberty was crushed to death between two branches.

Another young girl became a sacrifice to the gods of the harvest in Ghana, where she was impaled alive soon after the spring equinox. Sheep, goats, yams, maize and plantains were sacrificed at the same time and were hung up on stakes next to the girl.

Ancestors, who were also the recipients of sacrifices, occupied an extremely important place in African religions, especially among the Bantu in the central Niger-Congo region. Ancestors were looked on as guardians, protectors of tradition and morality, custodians of the land and judges of the living, meting out punishment for crimes and transgressions. Regular offerings of food, drink and presents were made to ancestors and it was the custom among the Ibo of southeast Nigeria to refrain from eating or drinking until a portion of a meal was laid on the ground or lodged at the ancestors' shrine. Elsewhere along the west coast of Africa, in Sierra Leone, the ancestral offerings consisted of rice and water. Among the Akan of the Guinea coast, also in west Africa, special rites took place every three weeks and a full-scale festival, the Odwera, was held each year in honour of the ancestors.

The religious ideas, the concept of gods and spirits and the principles of ancestor worship and sacrifice were transplanted to America from the west coast of Africa and from some way into the interior during the seventeenth and eighteenth centuries, when European slave traders kidnapped men, women and children or purchased them from local chiefs. These unfortunates lost everything it was possible to lose – home, family, native land, freedom – to provide slave labour for the plantations of the American South or European estates on islands in the Caribbean. What could not be taken from them, however, were their age-old beliefs and customs which remained undisturbed even after they were converted to Christianity.

From this, there emerged new Afro-American religions in which Christian principles were adopted in the existing body of beliefs, but never dominated them. Though the best known was Vodun, popularly known as Voodoo, which carried a large element of Yoruba beliefs from Dahomey, other faiths arising from African sources won numerous

Yoruba shrine figurine with offering, W. Africa.

Werner Forman

adherents, including Santeria, Candomblé, Macumba, Umbanda and other smaller cults.

For obvious reasons, the slaves made a secret of their African beliefs and rituals, but these were well enough known to slave owners and officials in the American colonies and around the Caribbean. Roman Catholic missionaries and ministers were especially disturbed by this development, which diluted their Christian message and, in their eyes, put the Son of God to the service of the Devil. Vodun bore the brunt of the persecution that ensued. In Haiti where it first became well established, the French colonial rulers considered Vodun to be a danger to their power. All African religious practices were banned and adherents of Vodun were imprisoned, beaten and executed. Many Vodun priests were among the victims, and they were, in addition, tortured for confessions. Vodun shrines were extensively destroyed. All this did was to drive Vodun underground where devotees continued to venerate their ancestors, worship their own gods and spirits and perform sacrifices while at the same time attending the Catholic Mass.

Vodun survived, and though it became most deeply rooted in Haiti, the religion was also practised in the Dominican Republic, the adjacent territory on the island of Hispaniola. Consequently, the fight against Vodun went on unabated throughout the nineteenth century. The modern weapons were insidious. Lurid propaganda was used to blacken the name of Vodun when, in 1886, a sensational book, *Hayti, or the Black Republic* by Sir Spencer St John was published depicting it as an evil religion in which human sacrifice and cannibalism were performed. Much of the author's information was apparently taken from Vodun priests under torture. St John was a British diplomat who came to Haiti with a British delegation and spent twelve or fourteen years there between 1863 and around 1877. He had been only four years in the country before he began writing *The Black Republic*. St John's claims that Vodun sanctioned cannibalism produced an outcry of horror – and a great deal of curiosity. So much so that, St John claimed, he studied the subject again and in the second edition of his book came up with a much longer, even more damning indictment.

In around 1932, fifty years after St John's book appeared, Hollywood took up this same theme with a series of frightening movies that left audiences in no doubt that Vodun was the religion of the Devil, motivated by the darkest of dark forces. Through this powerful popular influence, Vodun became a synonym for wickedness, evil, bizarre and frightening rituals and black magic. Not until proper anthropological studies were made in the mid-twentieth century was this image scientifically challenged, but films about the satanic powers of Vodun were still being made as late as 1987.

Unfortunately, some 'Voodoo' practices made it all too easy for the whole religion to be interpreted along the lines adopted by Spencer St John and other like-minded critics. Among some adherents of Vodun, there was a belief in zombies – a frequent subject of 'Voodoo' films – who apparently rose from the dead and, having no will of their own, 'lived' again as the tool of others. In New Orleans, followers of Vodun used to stick pins into special dolls as a curse on enemies or rivals. Magic as practised by the male priests, the *houngan* and the female, the *mambos* was 'white' and was used to promote good fortune and the healing of disease or injury, but the fact that some 'Voodoo' magic was 'black' tended to add fuel to the flames of opprobrium.

The name Vodun meant nothing more threatening than 'spirit' or 'divinity'. In the Yoruba language of west Africa, it meant 'mystery' and its beliefs reflected those of the Yoruba, Fon, Kongo and other west African tribes who brought it to America. Vodun beliefs centred round a chief god, Olorum, who delegated the creation of the world to a lesser deity called Obatala. As in Roman Catholicism, there was a body of saints, the *loa*. As in African animism, there were hundreds of spirits. Their collective names betray the history of Vodun. The original gods of Africa were known as *rada*. Those which arose in the New World were termed *petro*.

Animal sacrifices and gifts were offered as part of the ritual which contacted one of the spirits and asked favours. In Vodun, this was seen as an equable exchange. Worshippers provided the Loa with food and other items and in return, the loa provide protection, abundant crops, health and good luck.

Religious ceremonies featured the shaking of rattles, the beating of drums, chanting and dancing that built up to a peak of frenetic intensity until one of the dancers fell to the ground and became possessed by the loa. At that juncture, the dancer, in a trance, became the loa and was given all the honours due to the saint.

Sacrifices were offered in the form of a goat, a chicken, a sheep or a dog. There was, however, no butchery. The killing was done by a swift cut to the throat. From time to time, bulls were also used in sacrifice, usually only for special occasions. After sacrifice, the blood was collected and some of it was given to the loa to drink. The rest of the sacrifice was cooked and eaten by the participants in the ritual. One of the most important ideas behind Vodun sacrifice was a release of life to rejuvenate the *orisha*, the spirits, whose task of running the universe is hard and exhausting.

Vodun bore several resemblances to Santeria, the 'religion of the saints', more properly called *La Regla de Orisha Lukumi*, 'The Rule of the Lukumi Orishas'. There was the same belief in Olorun as the chief god, the sacrifice of animals and subsequent feasting, the possession of ritual dancers by a spirit and subsequent identification with that spirit. There was, though, a strong Roman Catholic input in Santeria which occurred after intermarriage took place between Spaniards and Africans in the New World. The orisha spirits in Santeria had their equivalents among the Catholic saints and Santeria deities were often represented by saintly images. Sacrifices in Santeria were offered directly to the orisha and as in Vodun, they consisted of goats, sheep, chickens and guinea hens. When a sacrifice was made, its blood was offered directly to the orisha in order to nourish the spirit. Sacrifices were also performed as a plea for divine aid in the curing of serious illness or bad fortune.

Unfortunately, like Vodun, Santeria and its practices became the subject of much misunderstanding, prejudice and a great deal of hysteria. In 1989, for instance, the bodies of five men were discovered at Matamoros, in Mexico and Santeria, together with Vodun, was blamed for the deaths. In the media, it was darkly hinted that they were the result of human sacrifice. Santeria was certainly involved, but not in the way the media was suggesting. The culprits were eventually found to be a gang of drug peddlers whose leader forced its members to watch a Hollywood film called *The Believers* no less than fourteen times. This horror movie, made in 1987, 'invented' a religion of its own, consisting of elements from Santeria, mixed with notions of human sacrifice.

Santeria centred at first in Cuba, a Spanish colony, while the very similar religion, Macumba, established itself in Brazil, which was ruled by Portugal in colonial times. In Macumba, which had several sects such as Candomblé and Umbanda, Roman Catholic saints and the Cross featured in worship, cocks were used as sacrificial animals and offerings of candles, flowers or cigars were made to the spirits. Macumba, also a syncretist religion, is not of very long standing. It originated in the mid-sixteenth century, at the very start of the slave trade, which ultimately brought some fifteen million Africans, and their religious beliefs, to the New World.

9

A Sacred Profusion: The Indian Subcontinent

Some 3,500 years ago, India was invaded from the area of present day Iran by the Aryans, whose name in Sanskrit meant 'noble'. Over a very long period of time, the Aryans transformed the beliefs of India and prefigured Hinduism, the oldest continuously-existing faith in the world. The Vedic faith of the invaders was written in ancient Sanskrit in the Vedas, a collection of texts setting down in fine detail various aspects of the Aryan religion. Of these Vedas, all of which are regarded by Hindus as divinely revealed and therefore sacred, the Yajurveda, the Veda of Sacrificial Formulae, contains instructions for performing sacrifices, together with verses for accompanying prayers.

As in many other cultures, sacrifice and prayer was an all-embracing activity in the Vedic faith. The performance of sacrifice was vital for the continuation of the cosmos and for controlling the passage from birth to life to life after death. Though its action might appear destructive, the purpose of sacrifice was regarded as creative and the primordial deity of India, Prajapat, Lord of Creatures, was constantly being regenerated in this way.

In more practical terms, the sacrifices had to cover a vast array of gods, demigods and demons, headed by the warlike Indra who had once vanquished the Sun, and after him, Varuna, guardian of cosmic and moral laws. The priestly caste, the Brahmins, conducted all religious ceremonies, which had, as their focus, the sacrifice of animals, and the rites of *soma*, an intoxicating drink made from the pressed stalks of the soma plant. The identity of this plant has remained uncertain, but it could be a species of ancient desert shrub, *Ephedra vulgaris*.

Vedic sacrifices in general were both complex and elaborate and offerings were on behalf of an individual *yajamana*, or sacrificer, who paid all the expenses involved. No sacrifices could proceed unless the wife of the yajana, the *yajamana-putni*, was present. Sacrifice could have many different purposes – as a plea for an increase in numbers of cattle, good luck, good health, long life, success, many sons – all accompanied by hymns and chanting designed to please the gods.

The yajamana selected sixteen *rtviks*, or priests to perform the sacrifices for him and to recite from the various Vedas. The four most prominent rtviks were the *hota*, who recited mantras from the Rigveda and actually performed the sacrifice, the *ugata* who sang hymns from the Samaveda and invoked the gods, the *adhvaryu* who chanted or murmured parts of the Yajurveda, and the chief priest, the Brahma, who saw to it that all procedures are properly performed. All rtviks had to be men of impeccable character and learning, all celibate and all thoroughly familiar with the Vedas. These exceptionally high standards were vital; for, to have their desired effect, all sacrifices had to be flawless and flawlessly performed. The Brahma, the highest-ranked among the rtviks, had to take on the mantle of a god for the purposes of sacrifice, simulating a new birth in order to do so: in a special hut representing the womb, he took up the embryonic position, wearing a belt to simulate the umbilical cord and the skin of a black antelope to represent the amnion and chorion, the membranes in which a foetus is wrapped during pregnancy. In early Vedic sacrifice, no temples or divine images were required. Ceremonies took place in the open air, in any suitable space which could be specially consecrated on important occasions. Altars were very simple, just a four-sided hollow in the ground or a small mound raised by piling on earth.

At home, where the domestic, *grhya*, sacrifices were performed, the hearth served as an 'altar' and offerings were made by the male head of the household, assisted by a priest. The grhya included the *mahayajna*, the five daily sacrifices, and those offered for special occasions, such as building a house or breeding cattle. Other domestic ceremonies, the

114

samskaras, were performed for every stage in the life of the worshipper, from conception and birth to death.

The public sacrifices, the *srauta* or *vaitanika*, by contrast, were major events requiring the services of at least five priests. Afterwards, there was usually a great feast of the *prasad* – food sanctified by being offered to the gods. The srauta, however, were not within the scope of men of modest means. Only kings, nobles or the very rich were able to afford the services of several priests, the sacrifices at the three fire-altars and the large number of days or even months it took for the ceremonies to be performed. Such feasts were not entirely a matter of pleasure and bodily satisfaction: they were a duty, and a fearful punishment was thought to await if it were not performed. This was laid down in the *Manusmriti*, the Laws of Manu, the first man in Indian mythology: 'He who performs the Yagna, but does not eat the sacrificial meat is condemned to be born as an animal whose meat he refuses to eat for twenty-one future rebirths.'

Fire was a vital ingredient in Vedic sacrifice. It was the medium that enabled Agni, the fire god, to transport the offerings heavenwards to the gods above. The *agnyadheya*, the installation of the fire, was an important ceremony in itself, so important that before it took place, the yajamana was required to fast. The Yajna, the fire-sacrifices, involved pouring out or throwing in food, grains, ghee or clarified butter, sandalwood and other offerings. Agni, who blazed in a special altar, the *kund*, made of bricks and mud, was regarded by the Aryans as the protector of the world. Propitiating him ensured their continuing prosperity and, perhaps even more important, avoidance of calamity.

One of the greatest of the Vedic public sacrifices involved *soma*, for which a *yajaman* had to be specially consecrated. This sacrifice had a very broad scope, incorporating the wellbeing of both gods and men. Using stones as a press, the juice was extracted from the stalks of the soma plant, then strained through the wool of a sheep and mixed with milk and water. The stalks were pressed three times, and before and after each pressing there were chants and recitations. Part of the juice was offered to the fire, the rest consumed by the priests. Several other offerings could be made, such as meat, milk, butter and cake made from barley. The milk or urine of a cow fed with the plant also qualified as soma.

Soma was no ordinary drink. A golden liquid, it was regarded as the ambrosia of the gods and the drink which gave them their immortality. The effects of soma produced ecstasy and high excitement and it was quite probably hallucinogenic. The religious poem, the *Bhagavad Gita*, the Song of God, written in around the second century AD, strongly hinted at this effect.

'Those who study the Vedas and drink the soma juice, seeking the heavenly planets . . . take birth on the planet of Indra, where they enjoy godly delights. . . . When they have thus enjoyed heavenly . . . pleasure, they return to this mortal planet again. Thus, through the Vedic principles, they achieve only flickering happiness.'[1]

Soma also had its earthly uses. It was said to fortify warriors in battle and enable poets to find the inspiration they needed to write verse. The fact that these abilities were produced, or at least heightened, by what was evidently a drug did not carry the opprobrium attached to such substances today. Rather, the effects of soma seemed apt, since the god of the same name, the deified representation of soma, was seen as the life-blood of all living things, including the sap of plants and trees. In ancient India, drinking soma allowed mere mortals to approach the exalted nature of gods, at least until the effects wore off, and the fact that it came about through ritual and sacrifice gave it validity.

Soma also served as the god of the moon, which was considered to be the cup which held the drink for the gods, as a heavenly bull, a bird, a giant rising from the sea and, of course, the lord of plants. The great god Indra was said to have drunk rivers of soma in order to obtain the strength to defeat the fearsome dragon Vritra, and Agni, too, was a copious consumer.

A variant of the soma ceremonies was Ashvamedha, the sacrifice of a horse which, like the youth masquerading as Tezcatlipoca in Aztec Mexico, was allowed a year of luxury before being ritually killed. The purpose of Ashvamedha was to celebrate the almighty power of kings, and ensure the prosperity of the kingdom. The horse in question was a superlative stallion which was allowed to roam anywhere it wanted for a year, carefully watched by a special royal guard. In its wanderings, the horse was regarded as a symbol of the Sun as it journeyed over Earth and, by inference, the power a king exercised over the world. The horse had considerable powers: if it entered a foreign land during its year of freedom, its royal owner had the right to demand that the ruler of that land fight for his freedom or submit to him. At the end of the year, the horse was brought back to the king's capital city and sacrificed at a splendid ceremony, which included prolonged banqueting and other festivities. The accomplishment of an Ashvamedha was a great milestone in the reign of a king in India: it enabled him to adopt the title of *cakravartin*, or universal monarch.

As time went on, however, Vedic rites, including sacrifice, became the victims of their own complexity. They took on the form of a religious bureaucracy that fed on its own complications and were hedged about with a mass of rules, which included specialized formulas and hymns. Ultimately, only the most experienced and learned priests were able to perform the rites and sacrifices properly, a development which separated them from popular comprehension and put them into the position of an élite. Even the Brahmas, it appears, were dissatisfied with this situation and an account in the *Mahabaratha*, the great Sanskrit epic poem, told of a king, Svetaki, who required so many yajnas during his reign that his rtviks began to grow restless. Although Svetaki paid them handsomely for their services, they refused to act as rtviks any more. Svetaki was able to find another priest to perform his sacrifices, but this story illustrates the dissatisfaction that occurred at a time when the new, more spiritual approach to religion characteristic of Hinduism was beginning to gain ground in India. The ultimate result was a religious reformation as profound as the break between Catholic and Protestant that occurred in Renaissance Europe two thousand years later.

The yagna sacrifices had many purposes, as a means of pleasing the gods, to indicate allegiance to the gods, or as a way of renouncing at least part of one's worldly goods. At heart, though, the yagna were too mundane and materialistic for the new spiritual ethos. They centred round worldly wants, personal satisfaction, desire for advantage and success and material gain. As the Vedic religion declined in India, in around 500BC, these things were becoming less important than *paramartha*, ultimate truth or *bhakti-marga*, the achievement of salvation, and similar spiritual goals.

Buddhism, founded between the fourth and sixth centuries BC by Siddhartha Gautama, was a very influential ingredient in this new mind-set. It introduced new ideas, revolutionary for their time – ideas of non-violence, universal love, peace, mutual understanding and toleration. The most crucial shift in the new religious thinking was Buddhist denial of the Vedas as a guiding authority in matters of faith. In particular, the Vedic blood sacrifices were the antithesis of *ahimsa*, the essential ethic of non-violence in Buddhism. The fact that sacrifices meant cruelty to animals was not the only point: it was becoming less and less acceptable for human beings to achieve their wants and needs in this brutal fashion.

In this context, Buddhism was basically a protest against the bloodletting, and a similar idea was at the core of other new philosophies that were gaining followings in India at around the same time. Ajivika, a sect founded by Goshala Maskariputra, and Jainism, founded by his friend Mahavira or Vardhamana, were ascetic in nature and devoted, like Buddhism, to non-violence and universal tolerance. Both, of course, were just as strongly against sacrificial practices. The Jains, in fact, used to build homes for old and diseased animals where they were lovingly tended until they died.

More secular interests in India in the sixth century BC had a strong stake in the new non-violent ideas. Originally, the yajna had probably been nothing more than the roasting of meat over fire in prehistoric times, when hunting and gathering was the only way it was possible to live. In time, this act of necessity became ritualized into sacrifice. Cows, bulls, horses and other animals which had once been merely prey now became offerings to the gods. However, once hunting and gathering as a way of life gave way to herding and pastoral or arable

An elaborate funeral pyre on the island of Bali, Indonesia, imparts the virtues of the sacred bull to the soul of the departed, at the same time providing a means of conveyance and wealth in the next world. (*Bob Krist*)

Richly painted wooden shields and a posy of artificial flowers, cigarettes and a plastic tub show continual offerings over many years at this shrine burial in Sulawesi, Indonesia. Honouring the dead with offerings is a universal compulsion, as became startlingly evident following the death in 1999 of Princess Diana. Flowers have also been found in Neanderthal burials. (*Albrecht G. Schaefer*)

Left: A ritualistic 'Skull burial' in the Celebes Islands, Indonesia. (*Chris Rainier*)

Below: Kwakwaka'wakw skull rattles from north-west America, near Seattle. The rattles are made from skulls which must have come from the severed heads of defeated enemy warriors. Many cultures around the world have believed that the possession of their enemies' heads gave them special powers. (*Seattle Art Museum*)

An altar dressed for worship in the Santerian religion, a close relative of Vodun, or Voodoo. The use of everyday objects elevated to the special status of ritual offerings parallels the Hindu concept of *Puja*. Santeria is growing in popularity, especially in the southern USA. (*Daniel Lainé*)

The burning of the Wicker Man. Captives of the Norsemen were imprisoned in a giant effigy of a man, made from woven saplings, and set ablaze at the winter solstice. The ceremony is commemorated each year in the Orkney Islands.

Vultures pick over the remains of human corpses, cut up by mourners for a Nepalese 'sky burial'. Individuals could stipulate that they wished their earthly remains to be disposed of in this way, as a 'gift' to nature; the symbolism of being carried to heaven in the crop of a bird has strong connotations with sky god sacrifices.

Below: In an atmosphere of reverent meditation, a Japanese Shinto priest prepares an offering. Eastern religion made an art form of the rituals that accompany even the smallest sacrifice. (*Chris Lisle*)

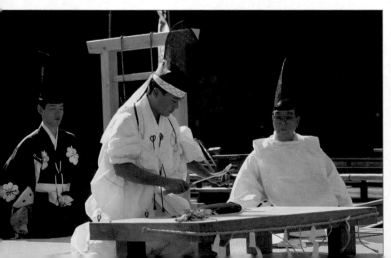

Cleansing is an important precursor to all sacrificial rites, nowhere more so than in India, where the banks of the sacred Mother Ganges witness daily public and private purification ceremonies. (*David Samuel Robbins*)

Opposite: Preserved in clay, these small handprints represent the last physical contacts with the world of upper-caste Hindu widows who committed themselves alive to the funeral pyres of their dead husbands. Outlawed in 1827, the practice of *Suttee* probably began in ancient times as religious sacrifice but later developed an economic imperative. This poignant memorial is in the fort at Jodhpur. (*Brian Vikander*)

Right: This terrifying painting from the Sikkim province of India depicts the goddess Hevajira as a hag wearing a tiara of skulls and a necklace of newly-severed heads. (*Lindsay Hebberd*)

Offerings for sale at a Hindu temple. (*David Cumming/Eye Ubiquitous*)

Above: A Jain, whose religious beliefs prevent him from taking any life, even insects, makes a fire offering at a shrine at Bahurbati, India. (*Chris Lisle*)

Right: Prayers printed on paper are sent up to heaven by fire in Taiwan. In Europe, children send demanding letters to Santa Claus up the chimney in much the same way. (*Michael S. Yamashita*)

Puja offerings from Khatmandu. Common to Indian religions, the practice of puja emphasizes the sacredness of everyday objects as ritual offerings. (See: www.hindunet.org for information). (*Craig Lovell*)

Below: Dayak men of Borneo/Kalimantan, once known as ferocious headhunters and cannibals, still make blood sacrifices. Here they are beheading a chicken. (*Charles & Josette Lenars*)

Women gather to make flower offerings at the *ashram* of a holy man in Orissa, India. (*Lindsay Hebberd*)

farming, the role of animals changed. Instead of being food, they were material assets and wealth. Cows and buffalo provided milk, or manure for fields of crops. The use of iron, that spread through the valley of the Ganges and elsewhere by around 700BC, made it possible to use more efficient tools to clear forests, or plough the land. In this context, draught animals became important and there seemed to be no sense in killing them as sacrifices.

Buddhism, Jainism and Ajivika had nothing to do with mundane commercial concerns as such, but their anti-sacrifice stance was very attractive to the farmers, traders and merchants who favoured and patronized them. Buddhism was the most amenable for agriculturalists, as opposed to Jainism which forbade the killing of insects and other pests and frowned on the ownership of land. Jainism was much more suited to trade, where there were no pests to be killed and no land to be owned. Agriculture, however, was the indispensable basis of national prosperity; which is why Buddhism received the most prestigious support from rulers and the nobility.

One of the most powerful proponents of Buddhism was the last of the Mauryan emperors, Ashoka. Ashoka came to the throne in about 265BC, and Buddhism changed his life in the most dramatic way possible. Originally a typically brutal royal conqueror and the author of many destructive wars, Ashoka was so sickened by the sufferings he had himself inflicted that in around 257BC, he renounced armed conquest. In its place, he embraced Buddhism and its principle of *dharma*, the 'right life' and spent the rest of his reign promoting honesty, fidelity, compassion, mercy, benevolence and non-violence towards animals.

The ancient Vedic faith attempted to modify itself to include the new ideas, but it gradually retreated. In time, the old practices of blood sacrifice were marginalized and the practice of vegetarianism evolved. The principle of sacrifice to the gods was far too deeply rooted to be entirely removed, and it was recast in bloodless, vegetarian form. The yajna rituals continued, but now a coconut was broken open to symbolize animal sacrifice or *pishtu-pashu*, miniature figures of bulls and horses, were used in their place. Beef was replaced by bovine

David Samuel Robbins

A cattle skull decorated with a prayer is offered among inscribed *Mani* stones by the roadside at Ladakh, northern India. The inscriptions are of the Buddhist mantra *Om mani padme hum*, offering prayers to the sky gods in one of the world's highest inhabited places.

products – the cowdung that once featured in sacrifice, together with the cow's urine, milk, curds and ghee. These were mixed together into a liquid called *pancha-gavya* but, in time, honey replaced the cowdung and sugar the cow's urine.

A further form of bloodless sacrifice, the *puja*, evolved in Hinduism with the use of flowers. Puja probably derived from an old Dravidian word from southern India – *puchey*, meaning 'flower action', though the sacrifices involved were not confined to blooms. The puja did not serve only to replace animal sacrifices, but made it possible for women to make offerings forbidden to them in Vedic times.

120

In its simplest form, puja consisted of daily quantities of flowers, leaves, rice, sweetmeats and water offered to the gods in temples or at home. At its most elaborate, when used in great communal festivities, the puja was a grand ritual comprising thirteen acts of worship. The deity in question was formally welcomed, offered a seat, had his feet washed with water and was offered more water mixed with sandalwood paste, vermilion and rice. Several separate gifts were then offered to him, first a drink made of honey, sugar and milk, then flowers, jewels, ornaments and clothes, a perfumed object, incense, rice, fruit, butter and sugar.

Blood sacrifices, however, were not entirely eliminated; and, in some instances, both puja and yajna in its unmodified form could be made to the same god. This was unsurprising when Hinduism incorporated paradoxical characteristics in some of their gods so that their manifestations were both beneficent, but also violent and destructive. Among them was Shiva, one of the three chief gods of the Hindu pantheon. Shiva was god of death and destruction yet at the same time he was the creator and the god of regeneration. Puja sacrifices were made to him at the festival of Shivaratri in the early spring, consisting of milk, curds, honey and ghee, bael leaves, fruits, or flowers. In his incarnation as Panchanana, Shiva became the healer of the sick, and barren women would offer sacrifices to him in hopes of having children. Yet Shiva also received blood sacrifices of rabbits, goats and birds.

Likewise, Kali, a name that meant 'black' in Sanskrit, was the evil aspect of Parvati, the chief Hindu goddess and also manifested herself as Gauri, the radiant mother goddess and protector. There were many temples in India dedicated to her, the most famous being the Khaligat in Calcutta. Kali was conceived as a terrifying, destructive deity and a goddess whose very appearance was loathsome to look upon. Her face was black and smeared with blood, her teeth were perennially bared, her tongue protruded horribly from her mouth and she had four hands which held a sword, a shield, a noose and the severed hand of a giant. In some of her images, Kali wore a necklace made of skulls or a girdle of severed hands. In Hindu mythology, Kali slaughtered her way across the cosmos killing all who stood in her path.

The goddess Kali, bearing implements of sacrifice. There is a curiously sensual quality to this otherwise fearsome Hindu deity, who inspired the notorious Thuggee sect of murderers until the British suppressed them in the mid-nineteenth century.

Werner Forman

Her insatiable taste for blood was said to have been aroused after she was summoned by the other Hindu gods to kill the demon Raktabija. The gods themselves had failed to dispose of Raktabija after every drop of his blood they shed turned into thousands of new demons just like him. In one version of the story, Kali solved the problem by pushing a spear through Raktabija's body, holding him up and catching his blood with her tongue. In another, Kali spread her tongue all over the battlefield and in this way prevented the demon's blood from reaching the ground. Either way, Raktabija was unable to reproduce himself and he died.

With these fearsome images in mind, it was hardly surprising that the Thuggee, a group of professional killers, were worshippers of Kali and made daily sacrifices of goats to her, supposedly to slake her thirst for blood. First heard of in 1356, the Thuggee, like their goddess, slaughtered their way across India for the next five centuries. First, they wormed their way into the confidence of travellers, who were considered by the Thuggee to be sacrifices to Kali. Then, before murdering them, the Thuggee would consecrate a pick-axe or *nishan*, which represented Kali's tooth, and make a special sacrifice of sugar. The Thuggee killed their victims by ritual strangulation with a noose or with white and yellow scarves called *roomals*, which represented the hem of Kali's dress. After stripping the body of its valuables, the Thuggee buried their victims in concealed places.

Many attempts were made to suppress the menace of the Thuggee, origin of our modern word 'thug', but success was not achieved, by the British, until the nineteenth century. It took six years, starting in 1831, and required close cooperation with several of the independent princely states of India before the Thuggee were finally brought under control. By 1837, 3,266 Thuggee had been captured, 412 of them were executed, 483 turned state's evidence and the rest were transported out of India or imprisoned for life. The British had broken the back of the Thuggee cult, but it was 1840 before they at last became extinct.

The British governor-general responsible for this success was Lord William Bentinck, who held office between 1828 and 1835, and ruled along lines in keeping with his own liberal beliefs. The fight against the Thuggee, however, was not the first time Bentinck encountered religious – or tradition-based – violence and sacrifice in India. In 1829, one of his first acts as governor-general was to abolish *suttee*, the practice of burning Hindu widows on their husbands' funeral pyres.

Suttee was a very ancient practice. It was so ancient that the place and functions of a living widow simply did not exist in the long-established social structures of India. Suttee was mentioned in the first century BC by the Greek writer Diodorus Siculus after his travels through the Punjab of northwest India but concrete evidence of the practice was not provided until much later, when memorials were raised to the women who died. The earliest of them was dated in the Indian calendar as the equivalent of AD510. Though suttee was in some part voluntary, its purpose fitted into the general picture of sacrifice as practised in Ancient Egypt and elsewhere: a widow, it was believed, died on the funeral pyre in order to accompany her dead husband into the next world. Suttee had great spiritual as well as social significance in India. When performed by a queen, it was a religious experience and a high honour for witnesses to look on her face, which in her husband's lifetime had been veiled, and watch her die.

Suttee could also occur while a husband was still alive, but was engaged in war. On the premise that he would be defeated and die in battle and might therefore not be cremated in the usual way, his wife underwent suttee on her own. In the twelfth century, however, a cynical reason for suttee emerged, as a way of getting rid of widows who had the right to inherit their husbands' property under the Dayabhaga law system of Bengal. In the sixteenth and seventeenth centuries, several attempts were made to ban suttee by the Mughal emperors of northern India, Humayan and his son Akbar, but it continued in spite of them. Even after the British apparently succeeded where the emperors had failed, suttee died hard. It continued for at least thirty years more and in the remotest parts of India, far from British official eyes, even longer than that.

Animals, too, continued to be used in blood sacrifices long after the establishment of Hinduism. One of these was the sacrifice of a frog in attempts to make rain. Frogs had the traditional reputation of being rain-charms because of the ability of their skins to absorb water. In the rain sacrifice, a frog would be placed in a pot filled with water collected from five different homes. The pot was then put in the large wooden bowl normally used to pound rice. On this occasion, the frog was crushed to death and, as it died, women would sing songs about the drought. Other 'frog' ceremonies stopped short of killing the creature. In northwestern India, a frog was hung on a tall bamboo with its mouth open so that the rain god would take pity on it as it croaked in fear and discomfort and grant rain so that its suffering might end. In other parts of India, frogs would be tied to an idol, or to a bamboo fan normally used for winnowing. Pouring water over the frog was meant to produce the desired rain.

While British disapproval or outright bans could not eliminate all sacrifices, they were able to modify them and make them symbolic and harmless rather than actual. For instance, after the British stepped in to forbid the unusual practice of finger sacrifice in southern India, a bloodless version appeared to keep up the tradition. In its original form, the birth of a grandchild had required the wife of the grandfather's eldest son to go to a temple to have the last two joints of the third and fourth fingers of her right hand amputated. The joints were taken off by a carpenter using a chisel. After this practice was forbidden by the British, the sacrifice was simulated by using flour paste to stick pieces of gold or silver to the fingers, or tying flowers round them, then placing a chisel over them and withdrawing it. The coverings were then pulled off, imitating the removal of the severed finger joints. In another version, gold wire was twisted round the fingers several times. The wire was afterwards removed by a carpenter who kept it as his fee.

Much more dramatic was the mock sacrifice that occurred when a Hindu was punished for killing or maltreating an ape, a bird of prey or a cobra while devotees of Vishnu, one of the chief Hindu gods, were present. The sacrifice in this case involved staging a resurrection. The culprit had a gash made in his arms and as loss of blood started to affect him, he fell to the ground as if dead. Blood was then taken from the leg of a Vishnu devotee and sprinkled on the 'dead' man's face. He revived and the resurrection was complete. In an alternative version, performed in southern India, the culprit would cut his own left forearm and smear the blood on his face. In other mock performances, this time in imitation of human sacrifice, live burials took place, complete with sacrificial fire and burnt offerings of plants.

Prohibiting the old sacrificial practices and watering them down until they were no more than charades had been a natural recourse for Lord William Bentinck and other humanitarians. They served in India with the best possible motives, but theirs were 'western' motives conceived by a foreign society with a totally different ethos and different social and political development. Bentinck's reforms in particular were afterwards cited as a cause of the Indian Mutiny of

Lindsay Hebberd

In a detail from a temple frieze at Kerala, an Indian warrior god receives tribute in the form of a severed head. Head offerings were common to many, apparently unconnected, cultures the world over.

1857–8, the last great – and futile – protest against westernization and the British assault on the ancient ways of India.

From the mutineers' point of view, the mock sacrifices, and the way British policy forced traditional religion underground or otherwise sought to change time-honoured practices, deeply affronted their most sacred beliefs. The British reformers achieved considerable success, if at great cost, but they never entirely eliminated the old traditions of faith and sacrifice. These continued to exert their power thousands of years after the Aryan invasions changed the spiritual face of India.

126

10

Steppes to Salvation: Central Asia and China

Asia, the largest continent in the world, has been the canvas for virtually every kind of belief. Shamanism was established there far back in prehistory, perhaps as much as 10,000 years ago, and the shamans served not only as intermediaries with the gods, but as diviners and healers as well. In China, strictly ordered state sacrifices developed separately from popular belief, as an arm of the ruling power, complete with much elaborate ceremony. Japanese Shinto was more of a folk-philosophy than a religion in the organized sense, but its devotion to the *kami*, the spirits that pervaded all aspects of life, was as much of a driving force as formal worship of a god or gods. Buddhism and its non-violent creed, arriving centuries before Christian missionaries or the armies of Islam, modified the religion of Japan and also had some effect in China, where the ethics of Confucius radically altered the tenor of society. In Asia, too, the practice of sacrifice covered the whole range of possible offerings, from human and animal to bloodless to symbolic sacrifice.

Certain isolated local sacrifices, usually blood sacrifices of great antiquity, played their part in Asian religious traditions: at Annam, in Vietnam, for instance, men were thrown alive into the sea in order to placate the deities who protected fishing. Well-born children were drowned in irrigation channels so that the rice-fields would receive sufficient water. In mountain districts of ancient Japan, a dog was killed by showering it with arrows before the gods were asked for changes in the prevailing climate: a black dog, whose colour simulated

127

but the cut must be clean and made with a single stroke or the sacrifice is not favourable. A libation of wine and water is poured on the altar or the sacrifice from a flat dish, which has to be held in the right hand, palm upward. After all the sacrifices and libations have been made, and the fire has died down, a sacred meal follows, accompanied by music and dance. This can be an exacting process: every single detail, every word of every prayer or incantation has to be right, or the sacrifice has to be abandoned and must start all over again.

The Internet is also the source of instructions for preparing and pouring the libation known as *blot*, the most sacred ritual in old Norse Asatru. Other websites detail shamanic offerings, though modern shamans confine themselves to sacrificing fresh fruits or vegetables, honey, milk, tobacco, small coins and incense. The principal quest of shamanism nevertheless remains to exert a favourable influence on the spirits through sacrifices and to ask for favours, protection or advantages.

Like many other neopagans, the neoclassicists have proved anxious to explain themselves and assure the public that their practices, in modern form, are a harmless means of celebrating Nature or of returning to the ancient spirituality which they regard as the true home of the human soul. This defensiveness is understandable, given the misunderstandings – genuine or otherwise – that surround the new practices. The pressure on neopagans has, however, made itself felt. Modern Druids may regard Stonehenge, on Salisbury Plain, as the place to celebrate the summer solstice and are willing to clash with the police to attain their objective, but many other neopagans resort to secrecy and perform their rituals privately for fear of discrimination or worse.

In this context, they can point to the statements made by US Representative Robert Barr in 1999 equating Wiccan witchcraft with the prevalence of youth violence in North America and calling for an end to toleration of Wiccan servicemen in the US army. George W. Bush Jr, now President of the United States, then Governor of Texas, challenged Barr's views and stated on radio that witchcraft was not a religion. Despite this, as well as recognition under the Civil Rights Act

Aboriginal Ainu people of northern Japan sacrifice a bear. The bear would be fêted and well fed throughout the year before being shot to death with arrows. This picture dates from the 1950s, but bear cults go back over 100,000 years to Neanderthal times. The modern shoes of the priest contrast oddly with the ceremonial barbarity of the occasion. (Hulton-Deutsch Collection)

black water-filled clouds, was killed if rain were required, and a white dog if the request was for sunshine and fine weather.

The meaning of the bear-sacrifice practised by the Ainu, the aboriginal people of Japan, on Yezo and Saghalien in the Kurile Islands was less obvious; all the more so, since, prior to killing the creature, they treated it with great honour, care and affection. A similar ceremony was performed every January in eastern Siberia by the Gilyak tribe. Quite possibly, these sacrifices reflected the respect accorded by prehistoric societies to the prey on which they relied for their own survival. The same approach occurred among the native Americans of the Great Plains in North America who apologized to their mainstay, the buffalo, before hunting and killing them.

The Ainu, likewise, relied on bears for food and clothing. Their attitude towards these creatures was intensely reverential. They placed bear skulls in a special place of honour in their homes and made them objects of worship. The skulls were also placed on sacred posts outside a house as *akoshiratki kamui*, or 'god-preservers', and received libations of millet beer or saké. The skulls of foxes received similar treatment: they were regarded as a protection against evil. The bear-sacrifice, however, was the most important religious ritual in the Ainu religion. From beginning to inevitable end, it could last up to three years, since the bear in question was captured as a young cub and was allowed to grow to maturity. During this time, the bear became a village pet and played with the children until it grew large and powerful enough to be dangerous. Then, it was confined in a wooden cage where it was fed on fish and a porridge made of millet. Just before the time came for sacrifice, people from the surrounding villages were invited to assemble before the bear's cage. The bear received an apology for its imminent death, with the assurance that the sacred *inao* sticks would accompany it into the next world for protection, together with cakes and saké wine so that it would not starve.

Like a condemned man, the bear was given a last meal. Then, it was let out of its cage secured with ropes, tied to a stake and strangled by compressing its neck between two wooden poles. An arrow was shot into the bear's heart, it was skinned and decapitated and its flesh was boiled and eaten. Roasting the flesh was taboo. Afterwards, the bear was included in the feast: some of its own flesh, together with millet dumplings and dried fish were placed under its snout. Failing to take part in the sacrificial feast was an extremely serious offence: it could result in excommunication from the Ainu community. Much the same fate as the bear's was accorded to eagles or hawks, who were reared in cages by the Ainu, then, with apologies and much reverence, sacrificed and eaten.[1]

Elsewhere in Asia, horses were regarded among the most noble of sacrifices. The fierce warrior Scythians, nomads who herded cattle and horses on the steppes of Russia north of the Black Sea, sacrificed large numbers of their horses for the funerals of their kings. In one Scythian burial mound at Ulsky in Kuban, southwestern Russia, 360 horses were buried with their master and his consort. Guards, servants and concubines were also present in his grave. The horses had been carefully preserved by having their internal organs removed. These were replaced with aromatic herbs, frankincense, and parsley and anise seeds. The horses' bodies were then coated with wax.

In contrast to these and other local or tribal customs, shamanism was a world-wide practice, appearing in the earliest times in all five continents. Among its many individual locations, it played an important part in the native religions of Malaya, where the shaman was involved in invoking the spirit of the tiger, and dominated the religious beliefs of the Eskimos. The main centre of shamanism was, however, in northern and central Asia. The name itself came from *saman*, a Manchu-Tungus word meaning 'he who knows'.

The shaman's first task was to go into a trance and become possessed by the gods. This was usually achieved by rhythmic dancing and not until this was done was he in a fit state to contact the gods, accompany the dead or the sacrifices to Heaven, make requests for favours and receive and transmit the divine replies. Through the entranced shaman, it was possible to acquire information on whether the next harvest would be successful or if disease, epidemics or some other misfortune were imminent, how disasters could be averted through sacrifices, and what these sacrifices should be. The ceremony was extremely elaborate and, among the Altai, might last for three days or more. Horse-sacrifice as featured in these shamanistic rituals (see Chapter 2) was only one way in which this form of ceremony was employed in Asian religion.

A Scythian belt-clasp in gold, depicting a horse being eaten alive by a winged lion, or gryphon. The Scythians were a Celtic people who inhabited what is now Romania from the seventh to the first centuries BC. They endowed their high-born dead with rich grave goods including sacrificed horses, possessions which had great military and economic value. (Archivo Iconografico SA)

A different use for horse-sacrifice, this time combined with the sacrifice of sheep, occurred in ancient Mongolia and elsewhere in central Asia, where it was used in funerary rites. The most spectacular took place at the obsequies of powerful rulers. These were occasions for great feasts at which animal sacrifices were extensive. In some cases, the horsemeat formed part of the feast while the rest of the animal was buried in the tomb.

In 1929 and 1947–9, Russian archaeologists excavated a burial site at Pazyryk, Kazakhstan, which had been used between the fifth and the third centuries BC by the Scythians of southern Russia and India. One of the tombs contained the bodies of ten horses, each killed by a single thrust from a dagger and buried outside the main funeral chamber. Other excavations revealed an even older burial site at Arjan, dating from the eighth century BC. Here, more than 160 horses, wearing full harness, had been sacrificed and interred. Despite the considerable age of these finds, this form of animal sacrifice still occurred in the nineteenth century. In 1860, the burial of a Kirghiz prince from the area south of present day Kazakhstan was accompanied by the sacrifice of 100 horses and 1,000 sheep.

Blood sacrifices did not, however, feature in Japanese Shinto once Buddhism, which arrived in the islands in the fifth century AD, infused the religion with *ahimsa*, its non-violent ethos. In Shinto, a basically animist religion which also included ancestor worship, hero and fertility cults, every living creature, object, social grouping or other natural and geographic feature had its own *kami*, or spirits. Forests were especially sacred. The word Shinto meant 'the way of the kami' and great care had to be taken not to offend them. For instance, in the art of paper-folding – Origami, which meant 'paper of the spirits' – the paper used was never cut out of respect for the spirit which had lived in the original tree.

The kami were so dominant in Japanese life that no move was ever made without consulting them. Before marrying or childbirth, going on a journey, fighting a battle or embarking on new ventures of any kind, the Japanese sought protection from their kami with ritual purifications, invocations, dances or the offer of gifts. In Japan, the number of protective spirits was infinite, for the dead themselves became kami and received daily sacrifices and offerings.

In the broader scenario of Imperial Japan, however, sacrifices played their part in the tribute owed to the emperor's court and government and were subject to official orders. While Nara and Fujiwara governments were in power, between the eighth and twelfth centuries

AD, the provinces had a duty to send animals to be used as sacrifices at the rite *Oho Nei*. Oho Nei was the origin of the three Rites of Great Sacrifice – the enthronement of the Japanese emperors, offering first fruits to the Imperial house, and the rites performed at the Ize Shrine in the south of Honshu island. Human sacrifices, too, were noted in the records of the time. In AD681, orders went out that each of the provinces must perform human sacrifice and a certain number of live humans had to be sent to the emperor for the same purpose.

Buddhism and ahimsa did not have an immediate effect on such practices, which continued for some time after this new non-violent faith was introduced into Japan. There was, though, one very early example of a more humane approach, in the late fifth century AD, when the Emperor Yuryaku ordered the setting up of a special department for the substitution of inanimate objects for blood sacrifice at the Ize Shrine. This idea took some time to become general policy. Official prohibition of blood sacrifices and the order to substitute pictures and effigies did not come until the end of the eighth century AD. Not long afterwards, iron or gold effigies were ordered for sacrifice instead of humans, and wooden horses were substituted for live animals in horse-sacrifice. Even the Japanese emperors lost their retinues in death when their households were replaced by clay figures. In time, as substitutions for blood sacrifice became standard in Japan, offerings consisted of rice, rice cakes, saké wine, fruits and vegetables in season and at shrines, small branches of the evergreen sacred tree.

Sacrifices had played their part in purification rites, but they were later replaced by bathing in cold water in winter among other 'harmless' ceremonies. Sprinkling salt was another substitute for the former sacrifices, as it was believed to clear an area of evil. Among other purposes, it was used to sanctify the mats on which sumo wrestling matches took place. A further alternative consisted of a paper image which was rubbed over the body and then thrown into a nearby river, on the premise that the water flow took impurities away.

Substitutions also affected the animal sacrifices performed at the Ontohsai festival. The festival was held each 15 April at the Suwa

Taisha, a Shinto shrine in the Nagano prefecture on Honshu, the largest of the four main islands of Japan. In a ritual reminiscent of Abraham's near-sacrifice of his son Isaac, a boy was tied to a wooden pillar, then placed on a carpet of bamboo. A Shinto priest approached, carrying a knife, and cut the pillar just as another priest intervened and the boy was freed. Afterwards, 75 deer were sacrificed. One of them was supposed to have a split ear, marking it out as a divinely selected animal. After the blood sacrifices were abandoned, the rites at Ontohsai continued, but with stuffed toy animals substituted for live animals. In time, as Buddhist influence spread in Japan, and vegetarian or inanimate sacrifices became the norm, the Japanese acquired a deep veneration for Nature.

Nature, of course, was controlled by the kami and honouring them could bring on rain, or make it stop or produce any other benefits that worshippers desired. In addition, the practice of sacrifice became practical as well as propitiatory as the Japanese came to regard themselves as providers of necessities for the kami. Everything they might need in their everyday lives was offered to the spirits – clothing, paper, textiles, tools, weapons, food, musical instruments, gaming boards and other means of entertainment, horses, carts and other types of transport.

The paper and textiles offered at the many shrines in Japan were called *gohei* and consisted of strips attached to a stick and carefully folded so that each side fell in the shape of a zigzag. Some Japanese considered the gohei to be the symbol of the kami and its presence in a shrine meant that the kami was there. *Shinsen* described the food offerings to the kami and, though varying from shrine to shrine, normally comprised rice, rice cakes, fish, meat, vegetables, seaweed, fruits, salt, water and saké. Of the three types of shinsen, *jukusen* described food that was cooked, *seizen*, food that was offered raw or *sosen*, food that was entirely vegetarian. At festival times, the first sheaves of rice or the first fruits were offered at shrines, but normally, shinsen was not meant for ordinary consumption. The food was specially grown for the sacrifice and only after it had been offered was it eaten by priests and worshippers who had attended the ceremony.

A public incense burner in a street in Japan. Aromatic smoke is a religious offering common to most cultures of the world.

Robert Holmes

One of the important festivals at which the kami received offerings with particularly elaborate ceremonies was Matsuri, taken from the Japanese term *matsuri-goto*, meaning 'affairs of religious festivals', or 'government'. Although offerings to and worship of the kami could take place anywhere, at any time and could be performed by individuals or families, Matsuri underlined the public nature of State Shinto, which became the official religion after 1868, when Japan was intensively modernized under the Emperor Meiji.

The first ceremony was purification, either by fasting, other forms of abstinence or by bathing in salt water. The kami were then invited to come down into the shrine by opening the inner doors, ringing bells and beating drums. Next, the shinsen were offered, together with cloth, papers, money, tools, jewels or weapons. Priests recited prayers and the worshippers offered the branches from a *tamagushi*, or sacred tree. After music and dances had been performed, the kami was asked to asked to withdraw and a great *naorai*, a feast, followed, in which the offerings of food and drink were consumed.

Shinto shrines were not, however, confined to Japanese temples and grand festive occasions. Miniature shrines, known as *kamidana*, or god-shelf, were also placed in individual shops and homes and here, water, saké, food and green twigs were offered to the kami every day. The kamidana were purely Shinto, but through the influence of Buddhism in Japan the Buddhist equivalent, the *butsudan*, was also installed in many Japanese homes and received offerings of incense and flowers. Another Shinto sacrificial altar, the *tamaya* was sometimes placed in homes in Japan for the purpose of worshipping the spirits of departed ancestors. Their names were inscribed on a *tamashiro*, or tablet, and when a death occurred in the family, the name of the newly deceased was added. Prayers and offerings were made to the kami every day for seven weeks, and afterwards the tamashiro was placed in the tamaya so that the recently departed could be worshipped along with all the other ancestors.

In China, as in Japan, popular worship was a very personal affair. At this level, Chinese religion was basically animist and centred around the favours that could be obtained by making sacrifices to the gods and spirits. This was the way to achieve freedom from floods, the recovery of stolen property and even pass marks in examinations. Good harvests, too, could be obtained by this means, and also by sacrificing to Hou Chi, Lord of Millet Grains. In Chinese homes, the most honoured place was the altar in the living room, which held a tablet listing the names of ancestors going back many generations. The head of each household, an 'emperor' in his own domain, had a duty to ensure that sacrifices were made to the dead on a regular basis.

Beyond everyday life in China, in the halls of the élite, sacrifices had a much more imposing face. China, too, went through its early stage of offering human sacrifices to the gods. During the rule of the Shang dynasty after the sixteenth century BC, humans were walled up in the foundations of buildings, possibly as part of consecration ceremonies. Human sacrifice was seen as evidence of prowess in war, and, as in ancient Japan, warfare was a constant occupation, with many prisoners captured. These served as victory offerings and afterwards, their heads were arranged within the grave of the triumphant military leader.

Sacrificing humans by burial in tombs was an ongoing practice. In 621BC, for example, the burial of Duke Mu of Qin state was thought to have been accompanied by 177 human sacrifices. Archaeological proof of this practice in ancient China was discovered in 1976, when the tomb of Fu hao, a consort of the Shang king, was excavated at Anyang, in Korea, once a Shang capital. The tomb revealed the remains of servants and prisoners, chariots with their horses and drivers, as well as hairpins made of bone and jade, 90 dagger axes and dozens of arrowheads, all designed to take members of the Shang royal family into the next world in the greatest possible splendour. Fu hao, it appears, was a warrior-general, who led 13,000 troops into battle against the rival Qiang, which possibly explains the presence of weapons and prisoners in her grave. The sacrifices were alive when they entered her tomb. They were led down a ramp into a pit and there they were killed. In 1977, the vast tomb of Duke Jing, great grandson of Duke Mu, was found at Fengxiang: it contained 166 human victims.

After Buddhist influences did away with blood sacrifices, these human offerings were replaced by wooden or terracotta figures. This did not, however, satisfy the great Chinese philosopher Confucius: he believed that even though no blood was shed, substituting images meant that humans were still regarded as disposable. The substitutions continued in spite of Confucius and led to one of the greatest, perhaps the greatest, archaeological find ever made: the Terracotta Army of 7,000 realistic, life-sized figures placed in the grave of the first Chinese emperor, Quin shihuangdi in the third century BC. It was found in 1974, by farmers digging a well at Lintong, in Shaanxi province.[2]

A Shang dynasty dagger-axe, discovered with grave goods in Korea. The design has phallic significance. (Royal Ontario Museum)

In later centuries, the Chinese emperors devised another level of sacrifice all their own when sacrifices – no longer human, but animal or inanimate – were turned into elaborate state functions governed by instructions from the imperial court. The most extensive of these state sacrifices, established by the first Ming emperor, T'sai tsu, after 1419, were not an original idea. State sacrifices had been performed as long before as the eighteenth century BC under the kings of the T'ang dynasty. T'sai tsu readily acknowledged his debt to these earlier rulers of China when he asserted:

'Since ancient times when virtuous rulers built their empires, nothing (was) more rigorously practised . . . than state sacrifices. . . .

Ritual wine jars and food vessels are among antiquarian grave goods commonly found in China and would have sustained the departed in the next world. (Royal Ontario Museum)

That is the way to communicate with the gods. Now, when I have received the mandate from heaven . . . and have unified the country, the first thing (to do) is to build the suburban altars and the ancestral temple to advocate the practice of ritual. My ministers, you shall select the appropriate (parts) of ancient and current practice. Make sure they are moderate and proper'.[3]

T'ai tsu, a thoroughly autocratic ruler, had seized the throne in 1368, and announced the nature of his rule in his reign title, *hongwu*, which meant 'vast military power'. T'ai tsu understood very well that one of the chief purposes of state sacrifice in ancient China had been to reinforce the status of the Emperor as the 'Son of Heaven' and with that, the authority and rights bestowed on him by the gods. By monopolizing the sacrifices that were due to the most important influences in life – the deities of the Sun, the Moon, the mountains, the seas and oceans and other elements – T'ai tsu also identified himself as the chief performer in fundamental rituals that would ensure the continuance of heavenly protection and favour. The sacrifices, which were accompanied by special religious music, were therefore a political move to enable T'ai tsu and his successors to buttress their political position through religion and its practices.

In formulating the Ming sacrifices, T'ai tsu took lessons from ancient mentors, not only the T'ang, but also the enlightened Song dynasty, which had revitalized China after AD960, after more than fifty years of political mayhem and violent lawlessness. However, though his motto was 'learn from the T'ang and Song', T'ai tsu's reforms were also influenced by Confucian principles of excellence. These principles served to set the highest possible standards of behaviour not only for his subjects, but also for the Emperor whose authority depended on conscientious performance of ritual.

Subsequently, a special government department, the Board of Rites, was set up to produce minutely detailed instructions on the performance of state rituals, and a Directorate of Sacrifices was formed to see to the practicalities. Directorate officials provided the implements the sacrifices required and assistance needed in performing them. The state sacrifices became the most important of the five court ceremonials, which also covered various celebrations, welcoming ceremonies for important foreign visitors, military parades and funerals.

Eventually, there were no fewer than forty-six distinct state sacrifices performed each year to honour Heaven, the Earth, illustrious or deified personages, natural forces such as the wind or thunder and various deities, such as the gods of banners and the military or the gods of the city. The imperial ancestors were given sacrifices of their own in the *taimiao*, the imperial temple compound. Further sacrifices were offered on important state occasions, such as coronations, weddings, before the inception of wars or when the Emperor embarked on a journey. The most important of all were the sacrifices offered by the emperor on the sacred Mount Tai in Shandong province: these rites marked the foundation of a new dynasty or the emperor's own attainments, and were made to request favour from Heaven and Earth for the new imperial house.

The forty-six sacrifices were classified in order of importance: thirteen were the ceremonials, or great state sacrifices, twenty-five were middle-ranking sacrifices and eight were small. The ceremonial sacrifices were distinguished from one another by the type of sacred jade offered, the colour of the sacrificial silk, the music that accompanied them or the numbers of the official escort accorded to those performing the rituals. Ceremonial sacrifice also included oxen, pigs and goats as the appropriate blood offerings.

Middle-grade sacrifices, such as those offered to the founders of agriculture in China or the innovator of silk manufacture and, perhaps surprisingly, to Confucius himself, merited only the offering of pigs and goats. Even the size of the sacrificial altar showed the relative importance of the rituals: the altar for ceremonial sacrifices was longer. In addition, twenty-four different types of food, housed in the bamboo and wooden vessels, was reserved for sacrifices to the imperial ancestors. The Middle-grade sacrifices, by contrast, had to make do with only twenty kinds.

All types of state sacrifice in Ming China were subject to a strict timetable. Fifty days before the State Sacrifice to Heaven, for example, the Emperor was formally requested to officiate. Twenty days later, rehearsals for the music to accompany the sacrifice would begin. Two weeks after that, the ancestors were told by the emperor that he should inspect the sacrificial animals. Next, the participants in the sacrifice were given four days' notice that the regulation three days of abstention were about to commence. The Emperor offered incense to the ancestors

John Slater

Buried in 210BC, the 6,000-strong 'Terracotta Army' faithfully recreated in individual clay sculptures, at life-size, the entire Imperial guard of the Chinese emperor Quin shihuangdin, together with chariots and horses. The soldiers in this astonishing 'token' sacrifice were to protect his mortal remains on the journey to the afterlife.

two days before the Great Sacrifice and, next day, he left his palace for the altar compound.

At the Great Sacrifice to Heaven, three groups of deities were to receive offerings, and 'spirit-thrones' were placed on the altar at various levels to indicate their relative importance. Spirit-thrones for Heaven were installed at the top level, for the Sun and Moon on the second level. The planets and other heavenly bodies, together with the forces of wind and thunder, clouds and rain were allotted the third level. Offerings of wine, silk, jade, food, candles, incense and the animals to be sacrificed were installed in front of the spirit-thrones on which spirit-tablets were placed to indicate divine presence.

142

At midnight on the day of the Great Sacrifice, the emperor waited under a great canopy until the spirit-tablets were in place, then entered to put on full ritual regalia. Torches were kindled, the deities were welcomed, the musicians began to play and the emperor initiated the actual sacrifices by offering incense three times and, together with all the officials present, making his obeisances.

Eight more stages of the Great Sacrifice were now performed to the accompaniment of music, obeisances and blessings. The jade and silk were offered to the deities first, then came the sacrificial food, two offerings of wine and an offering of wine and meat. In the eighth stage, the Emperor and other participants bid farewell to the deities and all the documents, silk and food used during the Great Sacrifice were confined to the furnace. The ninth and last stage consisted of watching these items burn and once they were at least half-consumed, the ceremony came to an end. Afterwards, the Emperor took off his regalia and returned to his palace, where a great banquet was held and awards were given to the officials who had taken part in the ceremonies.[5]

Keren Su

Among the most elaborate religious complexes in the world, the 600-year-old 'Temple of Heaven' in Beijing includes the Hall of Prayer for Good Harvests, housing a sacrificial altar where offerings were made by the Chinese Emperor to the sky gods.

11

Invite to a Cook-Out: The Pacific Islands

The Pacific, the largest ocean in the world, is a very deceptive place. In 1513, Vasco Nuñez de Balboa, the Spanish explorer and the first European in modern times to see it, was certainly mistaken when he scanned its calm surface and gave the great ocean this peaceful name. It was impossible to discern the true nature of the Pacific from Balboa's lofty standpoint in Darien, the link in Panama between Central and South America, or to perceive that a more recent popular description – Ring of Fire – was much more appropriate. Far from being calm and peaceful, the Pacific contains numerous volcanic islands and is surrounded by an almost continuous chain of dangerous and active volcanoes. On a map of Japan, for instance, the sites of their cones almost obliterate the land area. Similarly, all the eight major and 124 minor islands of Hawaii are actually the peaks of underwater volcanoes. The 'paradise islands' of the tourist brochures are no paradise at all.

Arguably, there is nothing more terrifying in Nature than the effects of eruption and earthquake as the ground shakes and splits, humans, animals or buildings are swallowed up inside the Earth, and flaming magma burns everything in its path. This spectacle of rampant Nature at her most destructive has naturally had its effect on the traditional beliefs and religions of Oceania, the collective name for the Pacific islands. Some of the world's most fearsome pagan deities come from this area: Abere, an evil female demon from Melanesia who attacks men, Babamik, from New Guinea, an ogre who practises cannibalism and, after death, becomes the ancestor of crocodiles, Maahiuki, from Polynesia, goddess of fire and earthquakes, Ngendei the Fijian creator god who causes an earthquake every time he moves, Whaitiri, another Polynesian goddess and cannibal, Darago, from the Philippine Islands, who is believed to require yearly human sacrifices to stop the volcanoes from erupting.

A similar belief was held in the Sangi chain of islands in the western Pacific Ocean, where a child was taken from a neighbouring village and sacrificed each year to the spirit of the local volcano, again to prevent eruptions. This, though, was not a straightforward procedure, nor a private matter. The village priestess systematically tortured the child by cutting off its fingers, nose, ears and other parts of the body. Then, as the villagers watched, the child was sacrificed by plunging a knife into the chest and opening it up. The body was then dismembered, and the sacrifice was followed by a great feast and, for entertainment, a display of cock-fighting. The celebrations went on for over a week. This gruesome process was later discontinued and a wooden doll was cut apart in place of the child.

In a society where practices such as these took place, it was not surprising that religious belief in Oceania was thoroughly permeated with magic, sorcery, the supernatural and the presence of malevolent gods incarnate in humans, birds or animals. There was also a widespread belief throughout Oceania that the gods of war, such as the Hawaiian god Ku, required human sacrifice or *ika*. Ika was also the name given to fish sacrifices, which possibly recalled ancient times when fish were the main offerings at religious ceremonies.

The making of sacrifices was one of the functions of the shaman in Oceanic societies, where religion was basically animist. As elsewhere, the living, the inanimate, the workings of Nature, the features of the land, were all imbued with their own spirits, all of which could turn malevolent and needed to be pacified. On Rua Hui, Easter Island, even the relatively benign Makemake, creator of humans and god of fertility, required human sacrifices, and a skull representing him was placed on newly-sown land to ensure an abundant crop. Well-being, success in love, work or war, good health and luck were other results of successful sacrifices and prayers, although the most important gods could be approached only by the most important people, the kings and the chiefs.

These men could hardly have been more highly exalted. Their *mana* or sacred supernatural power was so great that if a commoner's shadow fell on one of them, a king or chief was polluted by it and the culprit had to die. This was why King Kamehameha II of Hawaii made such a profound impact in 1819, when he protested against restrictive religious practices by deliberately breaking the rules surrounding the ritual consumption of food. The king's crime, committed during a festival, was considered so heinous that the Hawaiian priests broke up the idols of the gods and burned the temple where the rites were taking place.

The young monarch, 22, had just succeeded to the throne and appeared to be taking the reforms of his father, Kamehameha I, one step further. Kamehameha I, the great king who unified the Hawaiian Islands in 1810, had forbidden human sacrifice, which was performed to increase the mana of rulers. It was the custom for the *kapu* system of laws and punishments to go into abeyance on the death of a king, but after a time, it was expected that his successor would reimpose them. This is what Kamehameha II refused to do. Instead, he allowed the period of freedom from kapu to continue, which meant, for instance, that the ban on men and women eating together would be permanently lifted and so would the prohibition on women entering sacred places.

This was not a surprising move on his part. Kamehameha II wanted to bring Hawaii into the modern world and to operate in similar ways to the royal families of Europe. He allowed the first Christian missionaries to come to Hawaii, though he did not go all the way to conversion himself: that would have meant sending away four of his five wives and giving up rum, which he had no intention of doing. Even so, traditionalists regarded the young king as a heretic and a blasphemer. It was not lost on them that, when he visited England in 1824, the first Hawaiian monarch to leave the islands, he and his wife both died from measles within a short time of their arrival.

A burial site in the Asaro caves, Papua New Guinea, home of the legendary Mud Men. Corpses of enemies slain or captured in battle were dismembered and ritually consumed before being thrown in a heap.

Chris Rainier

The iconoclasm of Kamehameha was not emulated in other Oceanic islands, even though the burden of religious practice was very great. Time, tradition and fear had created a veritable maze of rituals and preventative measures. Lengthy purifications were required prior to war, the observance of innumerable superstitions had to be observed, terrible punishments were imposed for violating even the lesser kapu, such as trespassing on a sacred grove, and fasting, abstinence or ritual seclusion were regular practices. The vengeance of angry spirits was taken for granted in this atmosphere and elaborate rites, including sacrifice, had to be performed to allay their fury.

On Sulawesi, one of the four Greater Sunda islands of Indonesia, for example, the spirit of the tree which furnished the woodwork of a new building had to be placated in case it was still present, or was, perhaps, hovering around waiting to punish those who had made it homeless. A goat, pig or buffalo was therefore killed and its blood smeared over the woodwork. Much more was required, though, if the building was a *lobo*, or spirit-house: in this case, a dog or chicken was killed so that its blood ran down both sides of the building, or a human might be taken up to the roof and sacrificed.

Human sacrifice took place, too, in Borneo, in the western Pacific. When a chief died, his slaves were killed and nailed to his coffin. Their purpose, as in other pagan societies elsewhere, was to accompany their master into the next world and row the canoe that would take him on his journey. This tradition became bloodless when wooden figures of a man and a woman were placed at the top and the foot of the dead chief's coffin during his lying-in-state before the funeral. Another male figure, made of wood, sat on top of the coffin to row the chief into the afterlife.

Across the Pacific, in the south-central area of the ocean, human sacrifices were offered in the Marquesas Islands to a class of deified men who were supposed to have supernatural power over the forces of Nature. These human-gods were ambiguous – they were both kindly and destructive. It was thought that they could bring about good harvests, or conversely, make the ground infertile. Striking people down with disease and death was another of their magic abilities. Naturally enough, they held the villages they inhabited in virtual thrall, even though they lived in seclusion and could not be approached by ordinary people. One very old man of this kind kept an altar in his house, which was sited inside an enclosure. The house was decorated with human skeletons, hung head down. It appears that this man-god could demand human sacrifices at will. He would sit on his verandah and ask for two or three at a time. No other god in the village received more sacrifices and the demands of this deified old man were never disobeyed.

DYAK MODE OF DRYING HEADS.

The Dayak people of Borneo/Kalimantan had their traditional methods of preparing sacrificial objects, as this early twentieth century illustration of heads being cured graphically depicts.

Meanwhile, half a world away, this South American Jivaro tribesman has 'prepared one earlier' and is proudly displaying its sleek coiffure and expert stitching.

Bettman

150

A similar god incarnate was worshipped by families on the islands of Samoa, in the south-central Pacific Ocean, usually in the form of a fish or other animal. Any slight or disrespect shown to this sacred animal had to be expunged by pretending to make a sacrifice of a member of the family involved. The offender lay down in an oven, which was cold, and was covered with leaves as if he or she were being baked.

The priests of Oceanic gods could be just as dangerous to life as the gods themselves. The priests of Aitu Langi, the Samoan gods of heaven, were believed to kill coconut or breadfruit trees simply by looking at them. A passing glance would do, and the trees died. Fonge and Toafa, two smooth, oblong stones which resided on a raised platform in one Samoan village, were thought to be the parents of Saato, the rain god. When the time came round for catching pigeons, offerings, consisting of taro and fish, were placed on these stones to ensure that no rain would ruin this popular sport. Similarly, searching for yams was preceded by an offering of vegetables to the Fonge and Toafa, and if anyone passed by carrying cooked food, the stones had to have their share. Samoan gods also received offerings of cooked food when prayers were addressed to them to avert disasters and ensure prosperity.

On occasion, a god could himself become a sacrifice. When the people of Opulu in western Samoa were driven from their island by invasion, they killed a 'yellow man' who was supposed to be the incarnation of a god. The invaders agreed to take this sacrifice as an offering to end the war and allowed the refugees to return to their island. Killing a divine, and therefore immortal, being might appear to be a contradiction in terms, but it was, in fact, practised in many parts of the pagan world.[1] This rite might even go some way towards explaining the death of the renowned English navigator, Captain James Cook, who died at Kealakekua Bay in 1779 at the hands of Hawaiians. Until then, they had treated him as one of their four main deities, Lono-i-ka-makahiki, god of peace and agriculture and reputedly the most loved of all the Hawaiian gods.

James Cook, born at Whitby in Yorkshire in 1728, was making his third voyage to the Pacific Ocean at the time of his death. A brilliant

The Death of Captain Cook by the Natives of Owhyhee.

Grainger delin et sculp

Published as the Act directs by C.Cooke, N.º17,Paternoster Row, Oct 31.1788.

Cook was received by the cannibalistic Hawaiians as the promised sky god, Lono, and fêted with offerings. They turned against him when they realized he could not be the god, as shown in Grainger's picture. Hacked to death at Kealakekua Bay after an argument over tools, Cook's dismembered corpse was ceremonially partly eaten and the rest distributed as 'holy relics'. (For a detailed account, visit www.ccsu.cwc.net)

explorer and cartographer, Cook had criss-crossed the Pacific in eleven years of exploration, reaching as far north as the future site of Vancouver, in western Canada and in the south, confronting the great ice walls and freezing mists of Antarctica. Sailing under the aegis of the Royal Society in London and the Admiralty, Cook first voyaged to the

Pacific in 1768, to transport astronomers who were to view the transit of Venus across the sun at Tahiti. A secondary, but actually much more important quest, was to find Terra Australis Incognita, the Unknown Southern Land which was supposed to 'balance' the land masses of the northern hemisphere. Terra Australis Incognita did not, in fact, exist.

Instead, Cook discovered the east coast of Australia, mapped New Zealand, successfully sailed through one of the world's greatest navigational hazards – the Great Barrier Reef off the coast of the future Queensland – and visited several of the Pacific islands. The Cook Islands in the south Pacific were among several places named after him in and around the Pacific.

During his final voyage of 1776–1779, Cook made his second visit to the Hawaiian Islands, arriving on 16 January 1779 at a particularly propitious time, during the annual *makahiki* festival in honour of Lono-i-ka-makahiki. This coincidence produced what turned out to be a fatal case of mistaken identity. The Hawaiians were not entirely unfamiliar with the European sailing vessels of their time, but they reinterpreted their features in their own religious terms. For example, one of the symbols of Lono was a white banner flown on crossbars. The Hawaiians identified this with the sails of Discovery and Resolution, the ships of Cook's expedition.

Somewhat to Cook's own astonishment, he and his officers and crew were greeted by up to 3,500 canoes and 10,000 Hawaiians, but they were clearly not welcoming them as human visitors. The Hawaiians lavished gifts on Cook, performed great ceremonies in his honour and in all other ways seemed to regard him as Lono incarnate. A pig was sacrificed and Cook was smeared with its fat and he was afterwards anointed with coconut oil, so confirming his divinity. Cook, who had always been meticulous in respecting native customs, responded by letting the Hawaiians on board his vessel Discovery. He gave them a tour of the ship, together with presents and for their benefit staged a display of fireworks. This overawed his visitors but quite possibly convinced them even more firmly that he was, indeed, their god.

After two weeks, Cook weighed anchor and left Hawaii to resume his explorations. For the Hawaiians, however, his departure meant something quite different. It tied in with the legend of Lono, an unhappy deity who wandered the Pacific after killing his wife in the mistaken belief that she had been unfaithful to him. Lono built a triangular shaped canoe and departed, promising to return at some time in the future. It was easy enough for the Hawaiians to believe that an eighteenth century vessel in full sail was, in fact, this canoe, especially after Cook came back to Hawaii in February 1779. He had been seeking, though he failed to find, the Northwest Passage across the far northern coast of Canada, a perennial quest of navigators for many years. However, to the Hawaiians, Cook's reappearance meant that the myth of Lono was complete.[2]

What they did not expect, however, was that Lono's 'canoe' would come back in such poor condition. Cook's ships had received a severe battering in the Arctic waters north of Canada, and the Hawaiians were puzzled that the great god Lono could have suffered such damage in his own realm. As a result, their attitude towards Cook became less reverential. They also became much more aggressive, and proceeded to steal metals and Discovery's cutter. This was not the first time the Hawaiians had thieved from Cook's ships, but now he lost patience and on 14 February, a Sunday, he went ashore with nine of his crew to demand the return of his cutter. Although the Hawaiians prostrated themselves before him when he came ashore, a skirmish developed on the beach and Captain Cook was clubbed, repeatedly knifed, half-drowned and battered about the head with a rock. He died, quite probably, when an iron dagger was sunk into his neck.

Afterwards, with great displays of grief and remorse, the Hawaiians treated Cook's body like a ritual sacrifice: according to a Hawaiian record, the *Moolelo Hawaii* of 1838, the sacrifice was first offered by the island king, Kalani'opu'u. The body was dismembered and part of the flesh was roasted over a fire and eaten. All Cook's grieving crewmen were able to retrieve was the flesh of one thigh and some bones, which were returned to them on board ship. Cook's head, which had apparently been beaten to pieces, was given to the son-in-law of the high priest. The leg-, arm- and lower jaw-bones, complete with teeth, were give to King Kalani'opu'u. King Kahemameha I of Hawaii received Cook's hair. To the Hawaiians, these were not just trophies: they were permeated with divine power. It seems, too, that Cook's bones were incorporated into an image and carried in procession around the island. Anyone who touched this image was put to death on the spot.[3] The Hawaiian circumstances of Cook's violent end seem to have given it the appearance of a blood sacrifice, though he was naturally mourned in England as a lost hero foully done to death by savages.

However, it was also true that in the eighteenth century, almost any Oceanic or Hawaiian religious rite would have appeared repellant from a Christian Anglo- or Euro-centric point of view. Until Cook and other European explorers ventured into the Pacific, very little was known, and less understood, about the native customs of the region. Even after the French philosopher Jean-Jacques Rousseau and Cook himself promoted the romantic idea of the innately good, uncorrupted 'noble savage', the Oceanic peoples were regarded as virtually sub-human beings who could find salvation only in Christianity. This was a renewal of the old rivalry between pagans and Christians, so that even the bloodless sacrifice of offerings wrapped in *ti* leaves, as practised in Hawaii, looked like just another example of heathen excess. All the more so because the sacrifice of a pig was included in the rites. These sacrifices were intended to keep evil spirits away, and at harvest time, the leaves could fill an entire *heiau*, or temple.

Sacrifice at harvest-time was, of course, only one among a great mass of rites that covered every situation in which Hawiians might find themselves.

All important activities began and ended with sacrifices. Instruction in *hula*, or dance, also included regular offerings on a special altar and the end of training was marked by the sacrifice of *ailolo*, in which an animal was sacrificed and its brain eaten. The significance here was that the brain represented the start of a dancer's career. During that career, every performance was preceded by similar sacrifice. Different rituals,

Horace Bristol

Astonishingly elaborate funeral pyres constructed by Balinese islanders, with animal and floral motifs. Many cultures have exposed or cremated their dead on raised platforms, presumably to allow their souls to reach heaven more easily, or as a consecration to the sky gods.

but all with the same purpose, attended training in sorcery, wrestling or dodging the spear.

The construction of houses or canoes was accompanied all the way by special sacrifices. The sacrifices began even before a tree was cut down for the construction, and each step to completion involved more. The ailolo performed when the canoe was completed involved eating the head of a sacrificial victim, not just its brains. Every voyage made by the canoe was, likewise, accompanied by sacrifices at the start and after the finish. Nets and lines for use in fishing, the building of fishponds, irrigation ditches and dams – these, too, were subject to stage by stage sacrifice. Sacrifices performed by fishermen included seasonal rites for the *opelu* and *aku* fish as well as offering the first catch to the gods This was one of several similar rites in which 'primogeniture' was marked by sacrifice in Hawaii – for example, a first-born child or animal, or the first crops – and no new batch of cooked food was eaten by a farmer or his family before the gods had been given their share. The first fruits were also subject to communal sacrifice in Hawaii at the *kapu* Makihiki, the new year and on special occasions, such as the end of a famine.

Offerings to avoid famine were one of the *Emalliu mai ai ke 'kua*, the propitiatory sacrifices, which were also performed for many other purposes: for fertility in the fields, to prevent volcanic eruptions, cure diseases, win battles or to have children. The hiapo, the first child born in a family, had a special importance as proof that the gods had granted the parents' fertility. The hiapo was taken as a sign that the parents could, and would, have more children, and as such, was consecrated to the gods. A *mohai pana'i*, or substitute offering of a pig, was made in place of the haipo. The same theme of 'first fruits' was involved when the first three victims in a battle were marked out as sacrifices to the gods or the first product of manufacture was likewise consecrated.

Sacrifices were also made for personal reasons in Hawaii, and the prayers accompanying them left no doubt as to what the sacrifices were or why they were being offered. One rather poetic example, addressed to the *'aumakua*, a personal god, usually an ancestor, concerned a sacrifice offered by a man named Puhi who wanted to be freed from misfortune:

'For the 'aumakua of the night, For the 'aumakua of the day, For the 'aumakua of the fire and the mountain, For the 'aumakua of the sea, For the 'aumakua of the fresh water. . . . Here is the pig. . . . Here is the chicken, here is the fish, here is the vegetable food. A sacrifice offered by Puhi as compensation for all the sins he has committed. Deliver. Put an end to all the misfortunes of your descendant. Take away the diseases of his body. Here is his compensation offered to you. . . . Come eat and recognize Puhi, who is making this sacrifice . . .'.4

The prayer was similar in the case of a farmer offering first fruits to the gods. Addressing the elements of Heaven, Earth and the ocean, the grant of life was requested for the king, the Hawaiian chiefs, the people, the farmer and his family and dependents.

A basic principle behind sacrifice in Hawaii was that it had to be made to the associated god in each case. A first child or first fish caught were regarded as the 'bodies' of these gods and to sacrifice to any other deity was considered sacrilege. Hawaiian gods and goddesses were believed to metamorphose into earthly forms of their own choice. The 'bodies' of Lono-i-ka-makahiki, for instance, were pigs and the *aholehole* fish. Since daily offerings on behalf of the family were made to Lono, one or other of these animals was sacrificed to him when a child was born. The pigs were, in fact, specially fattened for sacrifice as soon as the mother knew she was pregnant.

After sacrifice, the pig was eaten by the mother as a means of obtaining the *mana*, or potency, of Lono both for herself and for her child:

> The pig was cooked in the . . . oven and all the other foods were wrapped in ti leaves and steamed with it. A cup (of *kava*) was prepared and when the food was ready to serve, the (priest) cut off the tip of the snout of the pig, the tips of the ears, and the end of the tail, a piece from each of the four feet, and a piece from the liver, spleen and lungs and placed them in a dish for the mother. A bundle of *taro* tops and seafoods was also set apart for her. Then the (priest) offered a long prayer offering the essence of the food to the gods and making their blessing for the first-born and subsequent brothers and sisters. After the prayer, the mother ate the food set apart for her, and relatives and family friends ate the remaining food.5

The sacrifices suitable for Ku, the war god, consisted of coconuts and *alua* fish, and Kanaloa, the Hawaiian god of the ocean and all that it contained, received octopus or squid. The association of gods with specific sacrifices often came about through colour. Thunder gods, for example, received black animals as sacrifice in imitation of the black thunderclouds that preceded a storm. In temples, a similar match was made when male animals were sacrificed to male gods and goddesses received female sacrifices, for instance, the offering of sows.

Of the three domestic animals most often used in sacrifice – pigs, dogs and chickens – the most important, and frequent, was the pig. The Hawaiians had a curious, rather ambivalent, attitude towards pigs. On the one hand, they were household pets and ate some of the same food as their human owners. The bond was so close that in the Hawaiian islands, piglets, and also puppies, were sometimes suckled by human mothers. However, on another level, pigs are sufficiently like to humans to represent a parody of the human form, so that their use in sacrifice represents the obliteration of a mutant and all that was mock-human. In this context, the human making the sacrifice would be freed from his own animality.

The sacrifice of humans in Hawaii had quite different connotations. Here, sacrificed and sacrificer belonged to the same species, and a human offering to the gods was, in principle, intended to preserve their lives. The practice also acquired much greater importance than the 'everyday' animal sacrifice because of its wider purpose. Before the abolition of human sacrifice by Kamehameha I, *kapu puhi kanaka*, the 'privilege to burn men' was reserved to the king, who embodied the whole community, or to a priest representing him. It was designed to divert misfortunes that affected everyone: disaster, such as a volcanic eruption, epidemics of disease, or calamities that might come in the wake of bad omens. One such omen was an eclipse of the sun, a fairly frequent occurrence in Hawaii, which regularly stands in the path of totality. Human sacrifice also had its purifying effects. The victims were mainly criminals or rebels who had polluted the islands with their sins and their violence.[6] Sacrificing them achieved a dual purpose – ridding Hawaii of their evil presence and serving the gods at the same time.

12

New Age, New Fears: A Modern Perspective

Despite the long battle waged by Christianity and Islam in the past, paganism and its sacrifices have not been wiped out. The rivalry continues, though today the weapons, the adversaries and even the scene of battle have radically changed. It is no longer a matter of competing faiths fighting with the swords and spears of medieval warfare. Many of today's upholders of the ancient ways have eschewed blood sacrifice, but where it continues, as in some traditional societies and newer religions like Santeria or Vodun, its opponents are animal rights activists, anti-cruelty laws or individuals convinced that faith should have nothing to do with bloodletting.

Neopaganism, as practised in several western countries today, is a fairly recent innovation, dating from the mid-twentieth century. Its followers, such as Wiccans who follow pre-Celtic European rites, modern Druids and others who devote themselves to the practices of Ancient Rome, Greece or Egypt have taken up where their ancient predecessors left off, using old texts, old recipes for sacrificial ceremonies or old incantations and prayers.

The new church most under pressure, especially from Christianity, is the Satanic movement first set up in 1966 by Anton Szandor LaVey, a former circus artiste. Among the 'alternative' religions, Satanism takes a somewhat different path, though not the path ascribed to it by its vociferous opponents. Satanists categorically deny having any connection with the Christian Satan, the terror-figure of medieval times and still a potent force for fear today. However, contrary to their

161

popular horror image as child abusers, exponents of the Black Mass, sorcery and other 'devilish' practices, most Satanists eschew blood sacrifice of any kind. Far from treating them as altar-fodder for sacrifice, Satanists regard children and animals as the purest manifestations of the life force and therefore particularly precious. And far from worshipping the devil, they assert as their basic principle the essentially humanist belief that people are in charge of their own destiny and need no intercessor with God.

Asatru, the heathen Norse faith whose origins go back to antiquity, has a rather different view of human destiny and the meaning of life: it teaches that the human race is directly descended from the gods. Asatru has its modern devotees all over Scandinavia, other countries in Europe, Canada and twenty-four of the fifty states of the USA, and gained recognition as a legitimate faith in Iceland in 1972. Today, however, the old animal sacrifices are replaced by beer, juice or mead. As in ancient Scandinavia, modern adherents of the faith believe that those who die in battle are transported by the Valkyries to Valhalla. In Valhalla, they eat *särimner*, the flesh of a pig that is sacrificed every day and every day comes back to life.

This resurgence of age-old faith in its several forms seems to have been prompted by a growing disillusionment with mainstream religions which, neopagans feel, do not adequately deal with matters of ecology or spirituality. A further factor is the prevalent emphasis on materialism, its rewards and its satisfactions. Seeking a deeper meaning to life, many people have turned instead to the more mystical aspects of Judaism, early Christianity and Islam; some have gone on from there to embrace the Nature and spirit worship of ancient paganism.

In addition, the advent of *perestroika* in Russia and the subsequent collapse of the Soviet Union in 1991 has had worldwide implications for those still devoted to the age-old ways and their sacrifices. Before communism lost its grip in the wake of this collapse, Santerians in Cuba, for instance, and the shamanistic Khanties of western Siberia were both severely repressed by their communist governments. The Khanties, a Finno-Ugric people, still lead a traditional life in the ice

A modern-day descendant of the Maya prepares religious offerings at Chichimila, Yucatan.

Macduff Everton

and snow of Siberia, where temperatures can reach as low as minus 45 degrees centigrade. They rear reindeer, and survive by hunting and fishing, which makes sacrifice an important adjunct to success and therefore survival.

If this way of life and its practices was frowned on by the communists, the official change of attitude that came with the end of the Soviet Union was a complete volte-face. In 1997, a local official was invited to join in an ancient ceremony of sacrifice performed in woods close to the River Pim and helped to provide the Khanties with a horse and cow for the purpose. At the sacrifice, reindeer were killed and offered to the Mother of Fire. The reindeers' heads and hides, together with the hide of a horse, were laid out on the ground and the place of sacrifice was covered in banknotes thrown by the participants.

In another part of the woods, two reindeer and a cow were sacrificed and their hides and the cow's head were ritually laid out. In a third location, close to the river, the hide of a sacrificed reindeer was surrounded by conical gourds made of sheet metal. The souls of reindeer were offered to the Sun and the Moon and to the gods, including Pim-iki, the deity of the river. The subsequent ceremonies included a séance conducted by a shaman, in which vodka was offered to Torum, a sky god and later distributed among the worshippers. There were so many of them that three bottles of vodka had to be opened before everyone received their share. During the proceedings, the shaman danced, jumped, and played the drum, employing different rhythms and so creating an air of religious excitement.

Though the sacrificial rites at the River Pim were sanctioned by the authorities, and provoked considerable public interest in Russia, acceptance of the old ways has not been easy elsewhere. Inevitably, those who have taken the neo-pagan path have faced accusations of heresy, devil worship and in the case of the 'sacrificing' religions, barbarity. The weapons now used in this continuing war include a mass of publications and books, the law courts and the Internet. The Net in particular is lavishly used by the new heathens, as they sometimes prefer to be called.

As recently as 1994, a website was posted detailing neoclassical sacrifice as used in Ancient Greek rituals. Designed to fortify the bond between the gods and humans through a sacrificial meal, the details are extremely precise, outlining the dress to be worn, the type of altar, altar fire and sanctuary suitable for sacrifice, the procession to the altar and a step-by-step guide for the officiating priest. Offerings consist of meat, fruit, flowers, grains and vegetables and, as a substitute for ancient blood sacrifice, a cake in the shape of an animal sacred to the god being addressed. Fruit or flowers are burned in a censer or on the altar. A small piece of sacrificial meat or vegetable is cut and burned on the fire,

Latter-day Druids celebrate the summer solstice at Stonehenge. Built around 3000BC on Salisbury Plain, Stonehenge is one of the great enigmas of prehistory. Sacrificial site or solar clock, recent studies show it to have been extensively restored in the Victorian era.

of 1964 and the fact that Wicca has been declared a valid religion by at least two US District Courts, this type of prejudice has not gone away.

In the ongoing campaign to counter it, the American broadcaster Margo Adler, who became a Wiccan priestess in 1973, put the case for Wicca on the Religious Tolerance website:

'We are not evil. We don't harm or seduce people. We are not dangerous. We are ordinary people. . . . We have families, jobs, hopes and dreams. We are not a cult. This religion is not a joke. We are not what you think we are from looking at television. We are real. We laugh, we cry. We are serious. We have a sense of humour'.[1]

Nevertheless, the fact that neopagan practices can take place in a hostile, even hysterical atmosphere underlines the difficulties faced not only by Wiccans but other new 'heathens' as well. Santeria is a prominent example, even though it is a syncretistic religion that includes considerable Christian input. Santeria is widely practised in Cuba now that suppression by the Castro regime has come to an end. There are some 300,000 adherents in New York and an estimated million or more in Brazil. Most of the problems Santerians encounter arise from the animal sacrifices that are central to their observances.

These sacrifices are deemed essential by Santerians because without them, they would be unable to feed the *orishas*, the deity-guardians, or to ensure their own wellbeing, good luck or forgiveness for sins. Sacrifice is also required by Santerian purification rites and forms part of all their ceremonies except for healing and death rituals. Santerians normally perform their rites, including sacrifice, away from the public eye and only initiates are allowed to know its secrets.

Inevitably, this clandestine cloak has worked against public understanding of the faith and has fostered several objections to Santerian sacrifice that have reached the American law courts. One case, in 1993, went as far the Supreme Court of the United States. In Santeria, animals are killed for sacrifice by a swift piercing of the carotid artery, one of two arteries carrying blood to the head and neck. The animal's throat is not actually severed, instead, a four-inch knife is inserted between the throat and the vertebrae, where the artery is located. After sacrifice, the animals are cooked and eaten at a sacred meal. All the orishas in Santeria practice receive sacrifices, usually a sheep, goat, hen, rooster or pigeon, but for some of them, additional offerings are made of turtles, ducks or, in the case of the warrior gods, three opossums or more.

After the initial rites are over, the head of the sacrifice is buried before sunrise at a crossroads where, Santerians believe, it absorbs the power of the relevant god, Eleggua. A week later, it is disinterred and the empty hole in the ground is sanctified by the blood of three roosters. The carcasses of the sacrificed animals are then buried, together with other items used in the ritual, such as corn, bananas and sweets, and the hole is covered.[2]

In 1993, in one of several cases brought against Santerian sacrifice – the City of Hialeah, Florida versus the Church of the Lukumi Babalu Aye – the City maintained that the animal sacrifice and its subsequent procedures, which included the drinking of the sacrificial blood, were contrary to public morals, peace and safety. The sacrifice also contravened the Florida animal cruelty laws. In these terms, therefore, the City contended that a ban placed on such practices in Hialeah was valid and, having regard to the secret nature of Santerian worship, there was no alternative but total prohibition. The court found for the City of Hialeah, but the judgment was later reversed after the Church appealed against the verdict.

During the appeal proceedings, it transpired that the City's case had been 'gerrymandered' and was specifically designed to target the Santeria church and its animal sacrifices, while excluding other killings, for instance slaughtering for food purposes or for eradicating pests. That aside, the appeal court found that it was possible to protect public health and prevent cruelty to animals by means other than a ban on Santeria sacrifices. The Church, meanwhile, had maintained, inter alia, that its rights under the First Amendment to the Constitution, granting freedom of worship, had been contravened.

Subsequently, it was generally reckoned that success in this and other court cases has firmly established the legal credentials of Santeria. Some progress has been made, too, in more widespread acceptance of Vodun. Though a similar religion to Santeria, Vodun has fewer adherents – 60,000 worldwide – and a slightly different style of sacrifice. In Vodun, the throat of a sacrificial goat, sheep, chicken or dog is ritually slit and the blood is collected in a vessel. Afterwards, it may be drunk by the houngan or the mambo – the priest and priestess of Vodun – while in a trance. The purpose is to feed the loa, or 'saint', to whom worship is being addressed.

Vodun's horrifying image, so vigorously promoted by Hollywood films and other propaganda, still survives, however; and under the popular name of Voodoo, the faith is still widely feared as devil-worship. In addition, communism has always regarded religion of any kind as a dangerous rival to its own ethos. As well as in Cuba, Vodun was actively persecuted under the Marxist regime that came to power in the west African state of Benin in 1975. It has since been rehabilitated, however, and six years after the election of a democratic government in Benin in 1990, Vodun was proclaimed the country's official religion.

Voduns, like other neopagans, make great use of the Internet, where equipment for their practices, such as incense and Vodun dolls, together with spiritual guidance, can be purchased online. Even *jujus*, the amulets designed to keep evil away, feature in the shopping list. Once, they were regarded, quite erroneously, as instruments for casting wicked spells and working destructive magic. Now, they feature as goods alongside many others in the e-market, the world's most extensive selling point.

On another battlefield entirely, pagan beliefs that survived conversion by Christianity and Islam have run up against an even more powerful opponent: the modern, essentially secular, world, with its commercialism, its concept of progress, its technology and its frequent indifference to longstanding traditions. Very often, tradition has dashed itself against its power and its materialist preoccupations to little or no avail. This clash, which could not be more fundamental, was illustrated in one of the states of Malaysia where giant plantation schemes and logging operations threatened to ruin age-old land rights.

In 1999, inhabitants of the village of Ulu Niah in Sarawak were attempting to hold back the activities of the Sarawak Oil Palm Berhad (SOPB) plantations. Protests and petitions for a halt to the company's activities, or even a moratorium to destruction by bulldozer, met with no success. The village fruit trees and its food and cash crops had already been bulldozed out of existence as the SOPB replaced local farmland with an oil palm estate. Then four men, believed to be gangsters hired to terrorize Ulu Niah, arrived in the village. Fighting broke out and the four were killed. Nineteen villagers were arrested over the deaths and ended up in prison on murder charges. Eight of them were subsequently released without charge. The other eleven were put on trial in 2001 and, at the time of writing, there has not yet been a verdict.

The response in Ulu Niah was to revert to ancient ways. On 2 and 3 October 1999, the first *Gawai Kelingkang* for over fifty years was performed. Its purpose was to invoke the ancestral and warrior spirits in support of the prisoners and aid in the struggle against the SOPB. At the Gawai, ritual gifts were presented to the gods, a pig was sacrificed and the village elders performed a miring, in which food offerings were made to obtain the spirits' blessing. The ceremonies took place around a pillar, which represented a tree, and stretched from the floor to the ceiling of the village longhouse. Offerings of rice wine, eggs, rice and herbs were arranged around it, while a procession of elders approached the altar and the *mengap*, the chief priest, chanted invocations.

That same year, old traditions and old sacrifices again entered into a modern confrontation, the tortuous struggle between Hindu India and Muslim Pakistan over the ownership of Kashmir. Hindu–Muslim enmity was nothing new, of course: when India, the jewel in the crown of the Empire, was ruled by Britain, confrontations were frequent and, some say, were encouraged by the ruling power on the basis of 'divide and rule'. However, this particular argument was much more recent, beginning with independence in 1947. Despite several wars, skirmishes and threatening political posturings, the Kashmir question has never been resolved. Then, in 1999, an implied threat that Pakistan might use its nuclear weapons against India – they were not in place in either country at the time – was sufficient to provoke the Vishwa Hindu Parishad (VHP) the world's largest Hindu organisation, to stage state-wide Vedic *yajnas* in Bengal.

Their purpose was drive out the 'muslim devils' of the Pakistani intelligence agency, who were active in west Bengal, by burning sandalwood and ghee at 1,400 yajnas across the state. The yajnas were pilloried in the Indian press as 'foolish and idiotic' and, since the VHP-backed Bharatiya Janata Party was then contesting an election on a traditionalist Hindu platform, nefarious political motives were ascribed to the sacrifices. Even so, a remark by a VHP official was significant in this context: 'A religious campaign', he said, 'has a more long-lasting impact on the people than a political rally or demonstration.'

The VHP offerings were, of course, bloodless, and were conducted according to non-violent Hindu tradition going back over 2,500 years. Even so, animal sacrifices were still taking place in India towards the end of the twentieth century. In 1997, the Chamundi Express, which was travelling from Mysore to Bangalore in the Karnataka of western India, was several times halted on the line by employees of the railway company who performed puja beside the engine. This took place on Ayudh Puja, the festival when, traditionally, the tools of a trade receive worship and sacrifice. The sacrifice on the railway tracks involved killing a goat or sheep and smearing its blood over the engine so as to make it 'holy' and ensure its safe journey.

The following year, Geeta Manja, activist and advocate of *satyagraha*, non-violence, took steps to prevent a repetition. The animal sacrifice was halted after she handed a copy of the Karnataka Prevention of Animal Sacrifices Act of 1959 to the engine driver before he took the train out of Mysore station. The ceremony went ahead, but only bloodless sacrifice was used.

The Karnataka was the site of blood sacrifice several more times during the 1990s as activists combated traditional rites conducted in villages in the area close to Mysore and villagers vigorously stood by their practices. At two villages, Voddarhalli and Machohalli, 18 km from Bangalore, birds and animals were sacrificed for *Makara Sankranthi*, the end of the harvest, after a hunt with shotguns, rifles and the beating of drums. Once caught, the animals were brought back to the villages tied to poles. The haul of sacrificial animals included a jungle cat, two jackals, several hares, a mongoose, fruit-bats, black-winged kites, herons, doves and a marsh harrier. At another village, Kadaballi, the prey, consisting of foxes, were not actually killed, but their ears were pierced to hold gold earrings and, after the ceremony at the local temple of Shiva, they were freed. Before this, though, firecrackers were attached to their tails.

Though the villagers of Kadaballi did not contravene the Karnataka Prevention of Animal Sacrifices Act of 1959, they were liable to charges of torturing the foxes under the Prevention of Cruelty to Animals Act of 1960. However, the Mali community of Badodara in Gujarat, western India, could have been charged with offences under both laws. The fact that they escaped prosecution seems to have been due either to official indifference or latent respect for the old ways – or both.

The Mali have practised blood sacrifice as part of their rituals for centuries. A large community, some 150,000 strong, they still believe that only the sacrifice of a goat can combat diseases, end quarrels, settle land disputes, cure childlessness and solve a host of other problems. However, according to one of their opponents, Pareshbhai Mali, scores of goats are slaughtered in a 'competitive show of devotion' and not always for religious reasons. 'They taste blood after killing the animal', Paresbhai has claimed.

Efforts to put a stop to the practice have provoked protests from the Mali that their religious rites are being infringed. To support this contention, a former Congress Party councillor and member of this community, Kalidas Mali, has claimed that all but five percent of the Mali support sacrifice. There have, however, been charges from opponents that many Mali are forced to kill animals under threat: if they fail to do so, they are told, their families will be wiped out.

As the law stands, and despite the efforts of activists and organizations such as the Gujarat Society for the Prevention of Cruelty to Animals (GSPCA), animal sacrifice remains legal in Gujarat as long as it is performed indoors and not at a public temple. Nevertheless, citing laws forbidding animal and bird sacrifices passed in 1972, as well as the Act of 1960, the GSPCA has urged the local police to stamp out the sacrifices. GSPCA members have raided two houses and rescued goats that were kept there as future offerings. To their dismay, though, they found the police response less than satisfactory: the Commissioner of Police sent out instructions to all stations not to register the sacrifices as offences and dubbed any future raids as illegal. The Mali, it appears, celebrated this 'victory' by sacrificing several goats.

Clearly, the old gods and their sacrifices, rooted further back in time than history knows, still have currency in the twenty-first century. Though persecuted and sidelined, challenged and ridiculed and, in some cases, deeply feared, their appeal persists, retaining the old loyalties as well as forging the new. Whether or not lobbies and laws can shift them from the subliminal depths of ancient belief remains unknown. It may never happen at all. Perhaps somewhere in the world there will always be those who stay faithful to the old ways and their sacrifices, and use them as the pathway leading to God.

Sources

Chapter 1

1. Frazer 228–53
2. Hubert & Mauss 2: 19–25
3. Ibid. 1:9

Chapter 2

1. Rudgley 221
2. Ibid. 223
3. Ibid. 216

Chapter 3

1. Frazer 266–8
2. 2 Kings 3:27
3. Ibid. 3: 24–7
4. Woolley (*Ur of the Chaldees: Excavations at Ur*)
5. Exodus 20:5
6. Genesis 22:9
7. Jeremiah 19:4–7
8. Numbers 8–17
9. Isaiah 66:3
10. Leviticus 1:4–9
11. Judges 11:31
12. Ibid. 11:34–5
13: Numbers 8:18
14. Numbers 16: 28–35
15. Samuel 15:22–3; Hosea 6:6; Amos 5: 21–5
16. Psalms 51:16–17

Chapter 4

1. Sauneron 144–5
2. Johnson 62
3. Ibid. 35
4. Davies/Friedman 187
5. Ibid. 188
6. Herodotus 94
7. Johnson 222
8. Herodotus 93–4
9. Ibid. 95–6

Chapter 5

1. Freeman 134–6
2. Jones/Pennick 12–14
3. Freeman 136–7
4. Cotterell 339
5. Hornblower/Spawforth 630–1

Chapter 6

1. Tertullian IX:95
2. Lucan 400–25
3. Cunliffe 191–2
4. Ellis 187
5. Cunliffe 192
6. Ibid. 185
7. Ibid. 196–7
8. Tacitus 42
9. Orosius IV.16:4
10. Jones/Pennick 120–1

11. Bede 2:15
12. Adam of Bremen Book IV
13. Johnes/Pennick 126–31
14. Owen 101
15. Jones/Pennick 140
16. Jurgela 41

Chapter 7

1. Lewis 59–60
2. Boturini
3. Davies 168–73
4. Diaz 229–330
5. Cortes 105
6. Ibid. 35–6
7. Drew 313–14
8. Cobo 110
9. Ibid. 112
10. Ibid. 115
11. Drew 385–95

Chapter 8

1. Mbiti 38
2. Ibid 58–61
3. Brett (*History Today*)
4. Qu'ran 22:36–7

5. Frazer 260
6. Ibid. 444–5

Chapter 9

1. Baghavad Gita 9:20–1

Chapter 10

1. Frazer 524–9
2. Paludan 24–5
3. T'ai tsu
4. Lam 115–27

Chapter 11

1. Frazer 223–521
2. Valeri 214–15
3. Ibid. 380
4. Ibid.53–4
5. Ibid. 59
6. Ibid. 37–83

Chapter 12

1. Neopagan religions (website)
2. Gonzalez–Wippler 160–1

Bibliography

Primary Sources

Adam of Bremen: *Gesta Hammaburensis Ecclesiae Pontificum* (History of the Archbishops of Hamburg–Bremen, Book IV).

Bede, The Venerable: *Ecclesiastical History of the English People*, Penguin Classics, 1990.

The Bhagavad Gita, Eknath Easwaran (ed.), Vintage Books, 2000.

Holy Bible (King James' Version).

Boturini, *Codex*, Libréria Anticuaria, Mexico City, 1944.

Castillo, Bernal Diaz de, *The Conquest of New Spain*, trans. J.M. Cohen, Penguin Classics, 1963.

Cobo, Father Bernabe, *Inca Religion and Customs*, trans. and ed. Roland Hamilton, University of Texas Press, 1997.

Cortes, Hernan, *Letters from Mexico*, Oxford University Press, 1972.

Herodotus, *Histories*, trans. George Rawlinson, Quality Paperback Book Club, New York, 1997.

Lucan, *Pharsalia*, Masters of Latin Literature, trans. Jane Wilson Joyce, Cornell University Press, NY 1993.

Orosius, Paulus, *Seven Books of History against the Pagans*, Book IV.16.4, trans. Roy DeFarrari, Catholic University of America Press, 1992.

The Qu'ran

Tacitus, *Agricola, Germany: Religion*: 9, trans. A.R. Birley, Oxford World Classics, OUP, 1999.

T'ai tsu, *T'ai tsu Gaohuangdi Shilu* (The Veritable Records of T'ai tsu), 26.1a, AD1419.

Tertullian, *De Spectaculis*, IX:95, Harvard University Press (1931), 7th edition 1992.

Modern Sources

Brett, Michael, 'Carthage, the God of Stone', *History Today*, February 1997.

Cotterell, Arthur, *The Pimlico Dictionary of Classical Civilizations*, London, Pimlico, 1998.

Cunliffe, Barry, *The Ancient Celts*, Oxford University Press, 1997.

Davies, Nigel, *The Aztecs*, London, Abacus, 1977.

Davies, Vivian & Renée Friedman, *Egypt*, London, British Museum Press, 1998.

Drew, David, *The Lost Chronicles of the Maya Kings*, London, Weidenfeld & Nicolson, 1999.

Ellis, Peter Berresford, *The Ancient World of the Celts*, Constable, 1998.

Frazer, Sir James G., *The Golden Bough: A Study in Magic and Religion*, Oxford University Press, 1998.

Freeman, Charles, *The Greek Achievement: The Foundation of the Western World*, London, Allen Lane/Penguin Press, 1999.

Gonzalez-Wippler, Migène, *The Santeria Experience*, Llewellyn Publications, 1992.

Hornblower, Simon and Anthony Spawforth (eds), *The Oxford Companion to Classical Civilization*, Oxford University Press, 1998.

Hubert, Henri & Marcel Mauss, *Sacrifice, Its Nature and Functions*, University of Chicago Press (Midway Reprint, 1998).

Johnson, Paul, *Civilisation of Ancient Egypt*, London, Weidenfeld & Nicolson 1978/1999.

Jones, Prudence and Nigel Pennick, *A History of Pagan Europe*, London, Routledge, 1998.

Jurgela, C., *History of the Lithuanian Nation*, Cultural Research Department, Lithuanian National Institute, 1948.

Lam, Joseph S.C., *State Sacrifices and Music in Ming China: Orthodoxy, Creativity and Expressiveness*, University of New York Press, 1998.

Lewis, Brenda Ralph, *The Aztecs*, Sutton Publishing Limited, 1999.

Mbiti, John S., *African Religions and Philosophy* (second edition) London, Heinemann Education 1989/1999.

Neopagan Religions (Internet website: www.religioustolerance.org/var_rel.htm).

Owen, G.R., *Rites and Religion of the Anglo-Saxons*, David & Charles, 1981.

Paludan, Ann, *Chronicle of the Chinese Emperors*, Thames and Hudson, 1998.

Rudgley, Richard, *Lost Civilisations of the Stone Age*, New York, Century, 1998.

Sauneron, Serge, *The Priests of Ancient Egypt*, trans. David Lorton, New York, Cornell University Press, 2000.

Valeri, Valerio, *Kingship and Sacrifice: Ritual and Society in Ancient Hawaii*, trans. Paula Wissing, University of Chicago Press, 1985.

Woolley, Leonard Charles, *Ur of the Chaldees*, Benn, 1929/1954.

Index

INDEX

INDEX